SCANDINAVIAN HISTORY

From the Ice Age to the Modern Day, The Histories of Denmark, Finland, Iceland, Norway, Sweden & The Vikings

HISTORY BROUGHT ALIVE

© Copyright 2023 - All rights reserved.

The content contained within this book may not be reproduced, duplicated, or transmitted without direct written permission from the author or the publisher.

Under no circumstances will any blame or legal responsibility be held against the publisher, or author, for any damages, reparation, or monetary loss due to the information contained within this book, either directly or indirectly.

Legal Notice:

This book is copyright protected. It is only for personal use. You cannot amend, distribute, sell, use, quote, or paraphrase any part, or the content within this book, without the consent of the author or publisher.

Disclaimer Notice:

Please note the information contained within this document is for educational and entertainment purposes only. All effort has been executed to present accurate, up-to-date, reliable, complete information. No warranties of any kind are declared or implied. Readers acknowledge that the author is not engaged in the rendering of legal, financial, medical, or professional advice. The content within this book has been derived from various sources. Please consult a licensed professional before attempting any techniques outlined in this book.

By reading this document, the reader agrees that under no circumstances is the author responsible for any losses, direct or indirect, that are incurred as a result of the use of the information contained within this document, including, but not limited to, errors, omissions, or inaccuracies.

FREE BONUS FROM HBA: EBOOK BUNDLE

Greetings!

First of all, thank you for reading our books. As fellow passionate readers of History and Mythology, we aim to create the very best books for our readers.

Now, we invite you to join our VIP list. As a welcome gift, we offer the History & Mythology Ebook Bundle below for free. Plus you can be the first to receive new books and exclusives! Remember it's 100% free to join.

Simply scan the QR code to join.

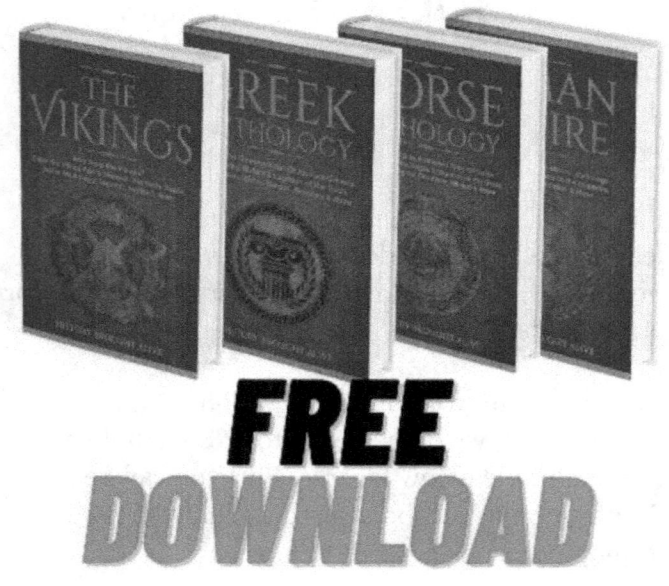

Keep up to date with us on:

YouTube: History Brought Alive

Facebook: History Brought Alive

www.historybroughtalive.com

CONTENTS

INTRODUCTION 1

CHAPTER 1: BEFORE THE VIKINGS 5

THE AESIR-VANIR WAR (MYTHS AND LEGENDS OF NORSE COSMOLOGY) 5
SCANDINAVIAN PREHISTORY & THE ROOTS OF NORSE CIVILIZATION 12
THE NON-NORDIC ORIGINS OF FINLAND AND ICELAND 15

CHAPTER 2: THE VIKING AGE 23

FROM LINDISFARNE TO THE DANELAW 25
ROLF THE GANGA AND THE AGE OF THE NORMANS 33
THE RISE AND FALL OF VIKING IRELAND 42
ON ICELAND 52
OF GREENLAND AND VINLAND 57

CHAPTER 3: THE CHRISTIAN VIKINGS AND THEIR SUCCESSORS 65

THE RISE OF RUS' 68
THE LAST VIKINGS 74
THE LIFE, ART, AND DEATH OF SNORRI STURLUSON 80
THREE KINGDOMS AND KALMAR 87

CHAPTER 4: THE RISE AND FALL OF THE SWEDISH EMPIRE 93

THE HOUSE OF VASA AND THE REFORMATION 95
NEW SWEDEN: RETURN TO VINLAND 105

THE DELUGE 110
THE GREAT NORTHERN WAR 114
THE END OF THE SWEDISH EMPIRE 118

CHAPTER 5: SCANDINAVIA IN THE MODERN WORLD 123

THE DANISH EMPIRE 125
MIGRATION AND INDUSTRIALIZATION 131
THE EXPLORATION OF GREENLAND 134
THREE NEW NATIONS 137
THE SECOND WORLD WAR 142
THE COLD WAR 151

CONCLUSION 159

REFERENCES 165

INTRODUCTION

Scandinavia is one of the most recognizable regions on the world stage, and is one of the most desirable destinations for tourists and migrants around the world. American leftists and liberals see Scandinavian countries as models for how to structure their society in the New World. Migrants from across the Middle East, Asia, North America, and even their nearby southern neighbors in Europe see Scandinavia as a staging ground to achieve their dreams: a place of security, opportunity, and freedom.

Somewhat ironically, Scandinavian countries, other than their modern reputation, are also famous for their historic reputation as the source of the Vikings. Modern media interpretations such as HBO's Game of Thrones (albeit using fantasy Vikings), The Northman (2022) starring Stellan Skarsgård, the History Channel's simply named Vikings, and video games like Age of Empires II and Hellblade: Senua's Sacrifice have helped to solidify this image of the Vikings as intelligent, gritty, and particularly dangerous warriors.

What is the relationship between the fearsome Vikings, who terrorized Europe for a generation (or more, as we shall see), and the progressive bastions of democratic governance, political freedom, and economic opportunity throughout the world?

This story is a popular one, but it should be noted that it is by no means unique. Spain is also a popular destination for both tourists and migrants of the 21st Century, but once ruled the world's first empire "on which the sun never set," pillaging peoples of at least three continents. Almost the same could be said for any European country: France, Germany, Italy, Portugal, the Netherlands, Belgium, even Switzerland.

Switzerland actually provides an interesting comparative example. Most people associate Switzerland with similar ideals to Scandinavian countries: progressive democratic governance, prosperous economic conditions, desirable places to live in the heart of Europe. The Swiss are also known for expensive chocolates and hand-made watches, marks of an affluent society. What people miss with Switzerland is a complex history of wars, political division, and mercenary-run statehood.

From this perspective, most people have a more complete picture of Scandinavian history, though the path from Viking raiders to modern nations remains a bit unclear. This book aims to chart that path in an introductory fashion, and hopefully spark interest in discovering a deeper and more comprehensive picture of the history of Northern Europe.

CHAPTER 1
BEFORE THE VIKINGS

The Aesir-Vanir War (Myths and Legends of Norse Cosmology)

At the beginning of the world there were two races of gods: the Aesir and the Vanir. They lived separately and in harmony.

One day a lone figure walked down the road on her way to Asgard. She entered the realm of the Aesir and began reading their futures. The Aesir were quickly amazed with her skills and abilities and began asking her all sorts of questions regarding their own futures and fates. Fate was a tricky thing as it was already set in stone, but small changes could be made, which to the Aesir, made all of the difference.

The sorceress promised to unweave the fate from its determined path and steer it towards the goals of her patrons. The Aesir, however, began to abuse her abilities and use her magic for their own petty grievances. Soon the Aesir were fighting among themselves, and when they had come to their senses, saw that the mysterious stranger who arrived unbidden to Asgard was pitting them against each other. The Aesir captured the sorceress and put her to the torch. Yet she was magical, if not divine, and though she burned thrice, she was thrice reborn from her own ashes.

The Aesir, realizing they had done all they could to punish her, released her and sent her out of Asgard.

Before she left their realm, the sorceress removed her guise and revealed herself to be Freya. And she was no mere sorceress, but one of the Vanir, sent there from Vanaheim to sow discord among their divine rivals. But now her mission, partial success, partial failure, had turned into a personal blood feud. She would not easily forgive the Aesir's attempted murder.

She returned to Vanaheim and told her cohorts the tale of the Aesir's cruelty and oppression. The host of Vanir rallied around her and they launched an assault on Asgard. The Vanir, whose divinity rested in subtle and profound magic, beat against the walls of Asgard, while the Aesir carried weapons of great might and brutality to fight off the attackers.

The war raged for eons. But just as Freya could not be burned to death, both clans of the gods realized that there would ultimately be no victory between them. They would need to reach a peace. In order to keep the peace, the Aesir and Vanir decided to first exchange hostages. The Vanir Freya, Freyr (her brother), and Njord (the Vanir lord of the sea), were sent to Asgard. The Aesir Honir and Mimir were sent to Vanaheim.

As it was custom, the gods treated their captives not merely as prisoners, but as guests. They were given seats at the tables with the rest of the gods, and in time, became members of their divine family. In Vanaheim, Mimir and Honir eventually rose from captives, to honored guests, and finally, to advisors honored for their wisdom.

Honir in particular became known for his wisdom. Every time the Vanir faced a challenging issue, they approached Honir for advice. But the Vanir noticed something odd. Whenever Mimir was absent, and Honir was approached for advice, he had a tendency to almost always answer, "Let someone else decide."

The Vanir came to find this suspicious. And after they carefully watched and investigated, found that Mimir whispered advice to Honir when the Vanir weren't looking. Outraged at this deception, the Vanir captured Mimir and cut off his head. They sent it to Asgard as a message of vengeance for fooling them with an unworthy hostage.

Upon receiving his clansman's head, Odin was distraught and wept. He had Mimir's head embalmed, and used his most potent magic to imbue it with the powers of speech.

Yet, this violence threatened to bring about another war. The Aesir and Vanir gathered again to prevent more shedding of divine blood. They sealed their peace with a spit oath: They each of them, Aesir and Vanir, chewed a berry and spit the juice into a bowl. Odin took the bowl, mixed it, and fermented the juice chewed by each of the gods.

And after it had fermented, the brew grew into the wisest being who ever lived: Kvasir.

Kvasir had many travels and adventures. In them he freely gave away his wisdom, seeing that it belonged to all. He used his wisdom to settle disputes and solve problems around the world. But on his last adventure, he was taken by surprise by a pair of dwarves. The dwarves lured him into a den where they asked him for his advice. But as soon as Kvasir's back had turned, they slew him, and drained his blood from his body.

The dwarves barrelled his blood and mixed it with honey. They didn't drink it, but hoarded it, and over time the blood of Kvasir fermented into a mead. While it was fermenting, the gods sought out Kvasir for his wisdom and advice. Yet he was nowhere to be found. When Odin came across the two dwarves, i.e. his murderers, they wept telling Odin the tale of how they witnessed the sacred Kvasir choke on his own wisdom.

But over time, on one of his own travels, Odin came across the fermented mead made of Kvasir's blood. Upon taking his first drink of it, he knew instantly what it was, and where it came from. Odin, fueled by the wisdom of Kvasir, brought poetry and song into the world. And these poems and songs became the Eddas which is how we know of the War between the Aesir and Vanir in the first place.

The Aesir-Vanir War likely never happened, but a popular explanation for origins of the myth is that it represents a fusion between one or more ancient tribes in Scandinavia, who first came together, failed at living together in peace, and then fought to a standstill until they became gradually more and more intertwined, socially, economically, and religiously (Lindow 2001, pp.

51-53). This is not a theory limited to Scandinavia, and is a common theory for explaining other mythological pantheons. Greek Mythology, for example, features its promiscuous central god Zeus who oft changes shape for romantic couplings with various goddesses, nymphs, mortals, and creatures. This is usually explained as the Greek cultural sphere (which held Zeus in high esteem) conquering, assimilating, and adopting the mythological elements from surrounding communities and cultures (Nilsson 1992, pp. 339).

It's possible that this also happened in Scandinavia, and that the Aesir-Vanir War is a surviving "record" of it, with one group holding the (proto-)Aesir and another holding the (proto-)Vanir as their primary religious figures. Other scholars caution us from this interpretation, as it could very much give a false impression of history by using an unverified oral history, centuries removed from the events they (theoretically) describe.

Still, from this most early period of Scandinavian history, we know that the Norse were connected to the outside world. Perhaps not as intimately as the empires of the Mediterranean and the Middle East, but their mythological framework was a part of a much bigger cultural sphere. To take Odin as a single example, he was the high god of the Angles and Saxons, who knew him as Wotan, and to Germanic peoples farther south as Wutan. Though it is far beyond the scope of this history of Scandinavia, the influence of the wider Germanic-Norse religion (known today in its reconstructed form as Asatru) lasted on Continental Europe long after the religion lost its political influence and most of its worshipers. The high German epic poem The Song of the Nibelungs (Niebelungelied) still holds many mythological elements in a deeply Christian Germany derived from pre-Christian Germanic mythology: an angry deity seizing a princess, forcing the hero to battle dragons over mountains to save her. The poem is one of the most inspirational sources of German cultural tradition, even carried into the modern day, inspiring Wagner to write an opera about it, where he drew even further into Germanic pre-Christian mythology. For our purposes, it simply shows that the lasting cultural background radiation from this vast mythological structure was wider and deeper than most people realize, and stretched far beyond the borders and time period of pre-Viking Norse Scandinavia.

Scandinavian Prehistory & The Roots of Norse Civilization

What we do know from archaeological records, linguistic evidence, and genetic studies is that Scandinavia has been home to human habitation for over 12,000 years (Nuse, 2018). And modern Scandinavians (relatively speaking) have inhabited the region stemming from migrations of people who spoke languages in the Indo-European Family. At some point around 500 BCE, somewhere in central or northern Europe, a group of Indo-European language speakers began to shift the way they spoke (Hawes, 2018. In the Proto-Beginning). Words with p's shifted into f sounds, f's became b's, b's became p's, c's, and k's, and qu's became hv's, wh's, and h's, and so on. We can see this change even today. Spanish "por que" is a distant cousin to the English "why." Closer to the period we are discussing, the Latin "pater" was cousin to the English "father," the German "vater," and the Norse "fader." This shift was the birth of the Germanic language family, including the Northern Germanic languages, which included the ancestors of Danish, Swedish, Norwegian, and Icelandic.

It is likely that the world that these proto-Germanic tribes inhabited was intensely local and very water-based. Though the Fenno-

Scandian Peninsula (the Peninsula on which Sweden, Norway, and Finland are located) is attached to Europe and accessible by land, the route is long, far, and winding. It is much more likely that the proto-Germanic peoples crossed from the Jutland Peninsula in Denmark, across the Danish Archipelago and onto southern Sweden (Price, 2015. p. 160). Even accounting for incredibly primitive watercraft, the distance between the Danish islands from Jutland to Scania often only requires crossing less than a kilometer of water to the opposite shore. Leaving Continental Europe from Jutland to Funen Island is only 811 meters, while the final leg of the journey from Zealand (the island on which sits Copenhagen) to the Scanian mainland is just over four kilometers at its narrowest point.

The peopling of the Danish Archipelago likely had a long-lasting effect on early Scandinavians. The constant crossing between islands and maintaining connections between tribal units all likely helped early Scandinavians look to the sea. Their skill with watercraft was something incredibly important from an early point in their history and development.

When the Roman Empire rose to become the dominant political and economic power in

Europe, Scandinavia was very much on the periphery of their mind and worldview, yet they were still aware of the these northern peoples, though whether this was through direct contact or through the more consistent contact they had with Germanic tribes closer to their own borders (in Germany and Belgium, for example) is not certain (Ó Hógáin, 2003. p. 131).

From archaeological evidence, we find that the early Norse (primarily in wet Denmark), like their Germanic cousins, and even more distant Celtic cousins, practiced "bog burials," committing some of their dead to the marshes, swamps, and wetlands rather than cremating them or burying them in the earth or at sea (Aldhouse-Green, 2015. Bog Bodies Uncovered). To the bogs they also committed valuables to send with them to the afterlife. And from the fourth and fifth centuries on, we find more valuables, especially silver and gold (Bursche, 2002. Circulation). This most likely points to Scandinavia being at the end of the long lines of trade which began with the Germanic tribes that plundered the Roman Empire in the 400s and brought the wealth northwards.

We also find that, after the final decline of the (Western) Roman Empire and the beginnings of the medieval period, gold and silver declined and became less common in Scandinavia (Burmeister, 2013. p. 56). One finds in archeological sites in Scandinavia that the Norse began using more bronze, and experimenting with more intricate drawings of animals.

It is possible that these experiences were important groundwork for the coming Viking Age. The sudden arrival (and subsequent departure) of abundance in their backwater region of Europe, and the knowledge that there existed prosperous, weak kingdoms out there for the plundering, likely made a mark on the Norse cultural psyche. Though we simply don't know: The early Norse, though they had an alphabet made of runes and were more literate than many of their contemporary societies, did not leave detailed records.

The Non-Nordic Origins of Finland and Iceland

Far to the northeastern end of the Baltic Sea is Finland. And on the other side of the North Sea, disconnected from the Scandinavian mainland entirely, is Iceland. Our inclusion of these countries as members of "the Nordic Countries" is historic, but their inclusion in the region's cultural-historical dynamic is relatively modern.

It may help in this section to try to get inside the ecumene (worldview) of the early Norse.

At the center of their framework of the universe was the sacred tree Yggdrasil. This holy tree connected nine worlds that spanned the universe, binding it together across time and space. Yggdrasil is what some scholars of religion and mythology (such as Mircea Eliade and Joseph Campbell) refer to as an axis mundi, a pillar on which the world ("world" broadly speaking) turns.

The first two worlds worth mentioning we've already discussed: Asgard and Vanaheim. Asgard, as mentioned, was the home to the Aesir, and Vanaheim to the Vanir.

There were also worlds home to supernatural beings that weren't the gods. Aelfheim was home to the light elves, and Svartalfheim to the dark elves. Myrkheim was home to the dwarves. Then there was Jotunheim, home to the jotuns. Commonly translated as "giants," the jotuns were the embodiment of chaos and disorder in the universe, opposed to the orderly universe that the gods protected and watched over. "Giant" is a poor translation for the jotuns because, in

Norse mythology, they are not simply large beings; they are mysterious, dark agents of chaos, who are sometimes large like tall men, and sometimes the size of mountains or more.

While Jotunheim was the home to the "normal" jotuns, there was also Niflheim and Musspellheim, home to the frost giants and the fire giants, respectively. Muspellheim was ruled over by Surtr, "the black," so called because he was like something burnt. Niflheim was ruled over by Hel. It is the name of this jotun from which we derive the English "hell" that represents the punishment for sinners in the Christian afterlife.

Finally there was Midgard. This was the world that the ancient Norse, as well as the reader of this book, would be the most familiar with. "Midgard" literally translates to "Middle Earth," i.e. the world in the middle of all of these strange, terrifying, and wondrous worlds. Our world.

But while Midgard was the world which the tellers of these myths and the writers of these poems could touch and feel with their hands, the rest of them were as real to the pagan Norse as heaven and hell are to modern Christians. And in their own strange way, these worlds reflected realities of the world the Norse inhabited, albeit metaphorically.

Iceland, a volcanic island at the northern edge of the Atlantic Ocean remained unpeopled until at least the sixth century (Parker, 2015. Notes: Chapter 4: Across the Atlantic). Like a combination of Muspellheim and Niflheim, Iceland remained a realm where ice and fire clashed. The fault line that continues to drive Europe and North America further apart to this day rose above the dark, salty Atlantic to form Iceland, where magma from the Earth's mantle violently spilled out onto the surface, only to cool into the waters of the Atlantic, and make the island a little bit bigger.

It is entirely possible that the first Icelanders were the Papar. The Papar were Christian monks who set sail northwards from the coast of Scotland, trusting to God to bring them to a promised land where they could devote their lives and spirits to their religion (Parker, 2015. Chapter 4). The land these Gaelic-speaking hermits found was Iceland.

There are some references to the Papar in early Sagas, including the Islendingabok by Ari Thorgilsson, who claims that the early Viking settlers encountered the Papar— although it was written in the 1200s, several centuries after the events it describes, modern archaeological evidence seems to point to some truth in the story (Þorgilsson, 2006. Chapter 1). Archaeological excavations in Kverkarhellir cave, on the southern coast of the island, indicate that people farmed in the area around the ninth century (just before or around the time the Norse began to explore the region) and found markings that are consistent with the depiction of crosses made in a contemporary Celtic style (Jarus, 2010). Though the Papar's effect on Iceland, if they had any at all, was minimal, it is a historic footnote that carries much of the mythology and contradictions of Icelandic history with it.

To the northeast, the early ancestors to the Sami and Finns practiced a semi-nomadic, primarily non-aquatic based existence, herding reindeer through the forests and lakes of the realm beyond or near the Arctic circle (Parker, 2015. Chapter 1). Here we need to bring up a matter of language. The word "barbarian" is derived from a Greek term barbaros, which translates literally to "babbler," (Harper, n.d.a). To the Greeks, a person who could not speak Greek was just someone who babbled. The mark of civilization was the Greek language.

Things like this still inhabit languages around the world. The Polish word for Germans, for example, is Niemiecki, derived from the Polish word for "mute." The Finnish word for Finland, Suomi, and the Nordic words for Finland, Finnland, are all of unclear origin. But the Nordic perception of the Finns, even to some extent in the modern world, is as silent, defensive foreigners (Khalimzoda, 2018).

This is a stereotyped image, largely dealing with more recent history (for example the Great Northern War, and Finland's domination by the Russian Empire for over a century), but while Finns today often speak Finnish, Swedish, English, and often some Russian, their reputation as a silent people remains—largely derived from their inclusion in the Nordic cultural sphere despite speaking a language from an entirely different language family.

Danish, Norwegian, Swedish, Icelandic, English, Italian, Spanish, Romanian, even Russian, Polish, Ukrainian, Farsi, Hindi, and Nepali are all members of the Indo-European language family, derived from early speakers living around the Caspian Sea who spread across Eurasia thousands of years ago. Another language family developed among a completely different group of people in the Ural Mountains. Around 5,000 years ago, speakers of the Uralic languages spread out from the Urals (Heršak,

2001). Some went farther north, some east, and some west. These westward-migrating Uralic peoples were the ancestors of the Sami, the Finns, and even the Magyars, who would settle Hungary in the last years of the ninth century and threaten the stability of Christian Europe. This culminated in the Battle of Lechfeld in 955 C.E., when King Otto the Great of Germany decisively defeated the Magyars, leading to the conversion of Hungary to Christianity a generation later.

For comparison, Spanish, French, Italian, Portuguese, and Romanian are all Romance language siblings, derived from dialects of Latin, originally spread by the Roman Empire. These languages began to diverge less than 2,000 years ago. Some have dialects that are more-or-less mutually intelligible, while others' differences are only visible in writing or structure. Magyar and Finnish languages diverged with the other Finno-Ugric languages nearly 5,000 years ago (Weber, 2019). Many of their similarities are visible only in linguistic structure.

In the same era as the Magyars threatened the long-term stability of Christian Europe, another group descended upon Europe's historic Roman center not on horseback from the steppes of Asia, but from the northern seas.

These were the Vikings.

CHAPTER 2
THE VIKING AGE

Off the east coast of Britannia, just barely out into the North Sea, is the Holy Island, where sits the monastery of Lindisfarne. Lindisfarne, in the eighth century, had become a hub of trade and a population center far outweighing its consideration today. This was partly owing to its location, and the ships that crossed the North Sea to trade in precious goods, fine religious objects, and fish, and partly due to the relics of St. Cuthbert, a famed holy man of the Celtic Church, whose final resting place was in Lindisfarne. Pilgrims from across Scotland and the Kingdom of Northumbria trekked the long routes across the British Isles to Holy Island to pay their respects and obtain blessings from the pious brethren who cared for the holy site.

But, in the first days of the year 793 C.E., there were bad omens literally in the air.

According to the Anglo-Saxon Chronicle (Killings, 1823. A.D. 793):

This year came dreadful fore-warnings over the land of the Northumbrians, terrifying the people most woefully: these were immense sheets of light rushing through the air, and whirlwinds, and fiery, dragons flying across the firmament. These tremendous tokens were soon followed by a great famine: and not long after, on the sixth day before the ides of January in the same year, the harrowing inroads of heathen men made lamentable havoc in the church of God in Holy-island, by rapine and slaughter.

Men from Scandinavia descended upon Lindisfarne and seized everything they could. Precious metals from religious objects, the jewels that decorated them, and even the robes worn by monks were torn from their bodies and used to haul their capture aboard the longships. Monks were wantonly slaughtered, with many pulled aboard the ships to be sold as slaves back in the homeland.

It was not a battle, but a raid. For the men the Norse attacked were not warriors, but scholars, more accustomed to copying down holy scripture, knowing little and less of the arts of war. Some of the monks held up crosses as a last-ditch effort. But to their attackers, the monks' god was dead, not even capable of saving Himself from execution. He was not alive like Odin, Thor, or Freyr.

One of the survivors of the attack was Bishop Higbald, who wrote to Alcuin of York, then at the Royal Court of the Emperor Charlemagne, and received a letter saying:

Pagans have desecrated God's sanctuary, shed the blood of Saints around the altar, laid waste to the house of our hope and trampled the bodies of the saints like dung in the streets. What assurance can the churches of Britain have if St. Cuthbert and so great a company of Saints do not defend their own? (Alcuin, 1974. Letter no. 26)

And so the Viking Age began. Across the British Isles and Western Europe, and certainly in other parts of the world in other languages, variants of the prayer, "A furore Normannorum nos libera, Domine" ("From the Northmen's Fury, O Lord, deliver us!") were heard (Parker, 2015. Introduction).

From Lindisfarne to the Danelaw

The men who went raiding to the Holy Island were not quite the first to do so. Sailing was a way of life for the Norse. The Anglo-Saxon Chronicle records earlier instances of violence conducted by the Northmen prior to the sack of Lindisfarne. In 787 three ships came from across the North Sea ("from the land of robbers," the text literally says) only to kill the reeve (the local magistrate). It seems that this attack did not leave a lasting impression on either the Anglo-Saxons, the Celts, or the Norse (Killings, 1823. A.D. 787).

These three northern European cultures lived in close proximity in the British Isles and the vicinity of the North Sea. The Northmen, prior to their centuries of raiding, were primarily traders who plied the waterways of Europe trading in cargo, from furs and slaves to the pottery and glass from al-Andalus (Islamic Spain), fine leather and carpets from the Mediterranean, and silver and gold everywhere (Parker, 2015. Chapter 2). It is not entirely clear to historians why the Norse made the shift from (relatively) peaceable trading to an era of fire and steel unleashed on their southern neighbors, though one leading theory is that with the rise of the Carolingian Dynasty (Charlemagne and his descendants) and the conquests and prosperity of the Islamic Golden Age, that there was much in the air for the Vikings to take to the sea seeking plunder and conquest (Ashby, 2015).

The British Isles had, until these centuries, a sort of backwater of Christendom. It was seen as the edge of civilization by the Romans, barely worth conquest. Their political descendants, the Anglo-Saxons, sought to subjugate and displace the indigenous Celtic inhabitants of Britain, and in the process there arose seven kingdoms in Britain. The most famous of these was Wessex, which would later grow into the Kingdom of England (the same Kingdom of England that still exists), but the one that ruled half of the east coast of England was Northumbria, which ruled over the Holy Island and the monastery of Lindisfarne.

Lindisfarne and the other monasteries of the British Isles were fond of creating "illuminated manuscripts." These manuscripts were usually copies of the Bible, decorated and illustrated with intricate drawings, and often painted with gold leaf. These creations were expensive endeavors, and were only possible in a society that had the wealth to sponsor their creation, to pay the men (monks), to educate them to study the Bible, and to have a population to spare on this kind of luxury rather than working the fields.

Implicitly and explicitly, Europe had achieved a new era of prosperity not seen since the days when Germanic plunder was filtering northwards during the fall of Rome. In other words, the wealth of Christendom was ripe for the picking. When those first ships returned home to Scandinavia, heavy with plunder, the Vikings on board hailed as heroes and warriors, the reward for further expeditions simply rose and rose. And as we shall see, the continued rise of the reward compared to the risk would only encourage the Vikings, who would go from prying jewels off the covers of illuminated manuscripts to seizing entire kingdoms.

Attacks were recorded in 794 on the Hebrides, a group of islands just off the west coast of Scotland. In 796 the Vikings attacked Jarrow, a town in the far north of the English countryside, but Northumbrian soldiers were able to successfully drive them off. Attacks only became more frequent. From the Norse perspective, history and mythology begin to mix uncomfortably. Ragnar Lodbrok ("Ragnar of the Hairy-Britches") was a particularly famous Viking, at this point more myth than man, who raided across the British Isles and the northern coast of Continental Europe. As legend has it, he was captured by the King Aelle of Northumbria, and refused to reveal his name. King Aelle cast him into a pit of snakes. From Ragnar's Saga, the Viking sang a death-song:

We swung our swords so long ago, when we walked in Gautland (Gotland)... since then people call me Hairy Britches (Lodbrok)... I stabbed the spear into the earth's loop... How the piglets would squeal if they knew the fate of the boar! (Parker, 2015. Chapter 2).

The "piglets", Ragnar's sons, had already cut a swath of glory and riches through the British Isles. But with the death of their father at the hands of the Northumbrian King, they decided that the only plunder that would satisfy their vengeance was the kingdom itself. In 865, the Great Heathen Army, led by Ragnar's sons Ivar the Boneless and Halfdan the Wide-Embracer, landed on the southeast coast of England (Adams, 2019. Chapter 3). The Army of Vikings stayed in Britain for over a decade, despoiling the landscape, looting at will, and installing puppet rulers and kings. They were in the process of founding a kingdom of their own.

Ragnar's son Halfdan settled his army around the city of York, agreeing to leave King Alfred ("the Great") alone in exchange for a Danegeld (Parker, 2015. Chapter 2). The "Danegeld", which was quickly becoming one of the most lucrative aspects of the Viking experience, was an amount of tribute paid to a raider and his forces not to attack. So while

Halfdan was pacified, he was not in command of the entire Army.

Guthram was a Danish Viking who originally asked his uncle to name him heir. Spurned for the crown of Denmark, Guthram joined the Great Heathen Army to carve out a kingdom of his own. Alfred paid him no Danegeld, and so he saw it as only right to continue his war. In 875, Guthram launched a new invasion of Wessex beginning with Cambridge (ibid.).

The war between Guthram's Vikings and Alfred's Wessex is known today for its brutality. Both sides had the upper hand at various times, and victories were followed quickly by stagnation and failure. At one point Guthram was backed into a corner, but Alfred's forces were unwilling to attack and risk such a devastating loss. Alfred conferred with Guthram, and they discussed a medieval equivalent of a ceasefire. In the discussions, Alfred made Guthram swear to keep the peace on a box of holy relics. A box of Christian bones meant absolutely nothing to Guthram, and he saw it as an easy price to pay. Alfred quickly recognized this blunder, and had Guthram swear on what he thought was a pagan item of devotion. But Guthram quickly agreed to swear on that, too. To quote what happened next from

Parker's The Northmen's Fury:

> [Guthram] felt himself no more bound by an oath sworn on a hallowed pagan object than he would have been by a promise made on a Christian relic, and he promptly moved to Exeter, ready to welcome the approaching fleet. This was, unfortunately for the Vikings, wrecked off Swanage with the loss of as many as 3,600 men. With adversity rather than piety weighing most heavily on his mind, Guthrum stuck to the terms of a new agreement and in autumn 877 withdrew his men from Wessex. (Chapter 2)

Alfred's failure to understand Norse culture and religion nearly destroyed his kingdom. But the running aground of the Viking fleet had saved his country... for a time. Believing his country safe during the winter, Alfred gathered his court for Christmas dinner, only to be attacked by Guthram's army. He escaped into the swamplands nearby, the war all but lost and Guthram's Norse Kingdom all but established.

Still, as long as Alfred lived, there was hope for the Kingdom of Wessex. Guthram's forces chased the Saxon soldiers into the marshes. But Alfred had not spent the intervening time idle, and he had regrouped, rearmed, and recruited more faithful Christians and loyal Saxons to his cause. They lured Guthram into a trap on Easter

Day 878. According to the Anglo-Saxon Chronicle,

> Then within one night he [King Alfred, and his army] went from this retreat to Hey; and within one night after he proceeded to [Edington]; and there fought with all the army, and put them to flight, riding after them as far as the fortress, where he remained a fortnight. (A.D. 878)

In other words: the Battle of Edington was a decisive victory for the Saxon army, and led directly to a peace on Alfred's terms. As the Chronicle continues,

> Then the army gave him hostages with many oaths, that they would go out of his kingdom. They told him also, that their king would receive baptism. And they acted accordingly; for in the course of three weeks after, King Guthrum, attended by some thirty of the worthiest men that were in the army, came to him at Aller, which is near Athelney, and there the king became his sponsor in baptism. (ibid.)

Guthram did not retreat and sail back to Denmark. In fact, he received exactly what he wanted: a kingdom of his own. Guthram and his Vikings settled in the eastern parts of England, bordering Alfred's Wessex to the south, and

Halfdan's conquests in the north. And to everyone's surprise, not only did Guthram keep the peace, he also held fast to his newfound Christianity.

The peace between Alfred and Guthram, and the Anglo-Saxons and Vikings more broadly, became known as the Danelaw. The Danelaw drew a line diagonally, from the northwest corner of England down to its southeast corner on the English Channel. To the north of the line marked territory that the Vikings (i.e. the Danes) were allowed to settle and live in peace, and to the south was reserved for the Anglo-Saxons (Adams, 2019. Chapter 4).

The Danelaw is still visible today on maps of England. While the language of "English" and the name "England" is derived from the Angles of the Anglo-Saxon kingdoms, one can compare place names, accent variations, and even genetic maps of modern England to see that there is a wide variation between north and south, right around where the peace between the Saxon kings of the south and the Norse kings of the north was drawn (Parker, 2015. Chapter 9).

Rolf the Ganga and the Age of the Normans

On Christmas Day in the year 800, King Charles of Frankia was crowned Emperor of the

Romans. His coronation marked the end of three-and-a-half centuries of relative chaos after the fall of the Western Roman Empire, and what was seen as an era of discord and disarray. The reestablishment of Roman order in the west was hailed as the dawn of a new era of peace and prosperity in Christendom.

It was not to be.

Emperor Charles, known to us by his French name Charlemagne ("Charles the Great") began an empire that would last over a thousand years, his actual descendants would not rule it for much longer. Charles the Great left his throne to Louis I "the Pious" who had three sons: Charles II, Lothair, and Louis II. Instead of granting two sons lesser titles and one son the entire Empire, he chose an old Frankish inheritance strategy to split the domain in an attempt to force the sons to cooperate (Parker, 2015. Chapter 1). To Charles, he gave "West Frankia," containing most of modern France, and to Louis, he gave "East Frankia," containing most of modern Germany. To Lothair, he granted "Middle Frankia," which has come to be known by the name "Lotharingia" and can still be seen in names around Europe such as the French province "Lorraine," or the country "Luxembourg," (Harper, n.d.b).

When Louis I died, his sons inherited their kingdoms and, instead of cooperating, immediately began competing with each other for territory and influence. Their favorite strategy was not open war (leaving their territory open for the other brothers to snag), but to pay third parties to attack their brothers' lands. Amid this chaos and disruption, who better to pay than the raiders who were already chomping at the bit to get a piece of the resurrected "Roman" Empire?

The reliance on royal raids began as early as 833, when Lothair encouraged the Viking Harald Klak to attack Frisia (Parker, 2015. Chronology). Lothair was apparently the pioneer of this strategy, and he even settled a fief to Harald in 841, less than a year after his father's death, and at the very beginning of the civil war against his brothers.

This was to become a theme that would change Europe forever.

In 845, Ragnar Lodbrok, he whose sons would ravage England and established the Danelaw, sailed up the Seine to sack Paris (Parker, 2015. Chapter 2). The sources are unclear (Killings, 1823. Endnotes, n.37). For starters, was it Ragnar Lodbrok? And secondly, did they succeed in sacking Paris? Or did they only sack a part of it... and make off with Danegeld?

As explained above, "Danegeld" became a common strategy in Christendom for Vikings to agree not to sack and raid and to be paid to go away instead (Richards, 2005. p. 169). Indeed, it could be where Halfdan first got the idea to leave Alfred's Wessex alone: his father's profit sailing up the Seine and making a lot of noise and threats, only to leave with a handsome pile of gold. But whether it began with the (semi-)mythical Ragnar in France, or later with his (very) real son Halfdan in England, once the phenomena of Danegeld began, it was very hard to stop. It became increasingly profitable for Viking raiders to show up looking fearsome, and then not risk losing men, ships, or reputation by having to actually fight.

For the Carolingian brothers, this took the form of paying the raiders to sack each other's cities, only for the Vikings to arrive at their goal and be paid a Danegeld to leave without a fight (Parker, 2015. Chapter 2). In other words, they were paid on their departure and then on their arrival, and went home without doing much of anything. Compared to sacking monasteries and terrorizing monks, holding cities and kings for ransom was far more profitable.

While it was a way to put out the fires of the northern raiders, and to scratch the itch of making their local fraternal enemies sweat, it was ultimately a mistake on the Carolingians' part. The Vikings took home Christian gold and used it to build up their communities (Richards, 2005. p. 169). But for the peasants and vassals of Europe, having these heathens in the halls of power only gave them more access to it. And paying them exorbitant sums of money so they could become intimate with the geography and waterways of the continent only served to make them more capable navigators and raiders when the Danegeld wasn't paid, or wasn't enough.

And this is where we come to Rolf the Ganga.

Rolf is often known by his latinized name "Rollo the Walker." He earned this name because, according to the Heimskringla, "he was of such great size that no horse could bear him, so he always journeyed on foot," (Chapter 24, Ganger-Hrólf Is Outlawed). In the late 9th Century, Rolf wanted to earn the glory and gold of sacking Paris, or at least just the gold of a Danegeld's worth to not sack the city. But the Parisians were not idle in the years between Ragnar's initial attack and Rolf's arrival. They spent the years building up the city's defenses. The male population of the city was ordered to build defensive works: including bridges, causeways, and fortresses. These ordinances also distributed garrison shifts. The strategy was aimed at not necessarily defeating the Vikings in open battle, but discouraging them by making their journey up the Seine arduous, difficult, and too bloody to be worth the Danegeld (or sacking) (Parker, 2015. Chapter 2). The pièce de résistance was the grand, imposing Pont de l'Arche. The bridge was built at the confluence of the Seine and the Eure and on either end was protected by fortresses.

This was the Frankia that Rolf found his Vikings facing. They besieged Paris in 885–6 but made no progress (Adams, 2019. Chapter 7. Fragmentary Annals). Growing restless and ready to leave, King Charles came to Rolf with an offer: He would pay Rolf and his men money not to return to the sea, but to pass Paris and sack Burgundy, which was under Lotharingian control. Hard to pass up a deal like that. So Rolf and his Vikings took the money and raided the Continent for 26 years.

Rolf and his Vikings returned to Charles's realm in 911. They began moving back towards Paris to an unclear end. On the way they passed through the city of Chartres, armed and ready for battle. Rolf decided to take the battle to the

Franks, but their nearly three decades of experience were not enough to match being vastly outnumbered by the Christians, and they had reports that King Charles himself would arrive soon with reinforcements.

The Vikings had to use their wits and trickery to overcome the enemy. Rolf had his men build a wall, not of stone or shields, but of sheep carcasses. The smell of blood terrified King Charles's cavalry, and broke the charge of his knights—the Franks' most powerful weapon—and ultimately turned the tide in the Vikings' favor (Extra Credits, 2018f). At least temporarily.

King Charles had seen his father and grandfather nearly beggar their realms by paying Danegeld to the Vikings. Rather than solve the problem of losing the wealth of the Kingdom to raiders, they were willingly giving it away for a false promise of safety. Instead, when he met with Rolf, no longer the young, spry Viking, but a wizened, old veteran, in 911 below the walls of Chartres, he had a new idea. Charles required merely that Rolf convert to Christianity, defend the realm, and pay regular tribute to the crown, and in return he could have a landed noble title of his own (Parker, 2015. Chapter 9).

These terms were agreeable to Rollo. Though he had some terms himself. He would pay Charles tribute and homage, but he refused to bow and kiss the king's feet. As Parker (2015) tells us, "one of Rollo's followers was chosen to enact this humiliating part of the proceedings, but the importunate stand-in seized Charles's foot, causing the king to topple over backwards" (ibid.).

The land given to Rolf and his men was at the mouth of the Seine. This land settled by Rolf and his Northmen was named after them: Normandy. And the Christianized Vikings who followed Rolf to their new homeland were forever known as Normans, though the historical record shows us that initially, there were some hiccups. These first Normans were baptized by Christian monks, but they "reverted to pagan practice whenever it suited them," (ibid.). And Rolf himself asked for both a Christian priest to confess to, as well as Christian slaves to be sacrificed to Odin and Thor, on his deathbed in 942. His son was absolutely a Christian, as were the immediate descendants of the other Viking settlers. Not only that, but as soon as Rolf became a vassal to King Charles, he almost immediately began playing politics, forging alliances and siding with Charles's rivals whenever it suited him politically.

This was a strategy that Rolf's descendants—indeed, the descendants of all of the Normans—would put to effect. This relatively small piece of land on the European continent, settled by veterans from a decades-long raid into modern France, would ultimately have profound ramifications in the succeeding centuries. Normans would go on to raid Italy, putting the city of Bari to siege multiple times. They would threaten to conquer the Eastern Roman Empire and put one of their own on the throne in Constantinople. They formed one of the largest contingents of soldiers in the first Crusades, and later would establish their own crusader states in the Holy Land.

The Heimskringla, a history of the Norwegian Kings written by Snorri Sturluson, has this to say about Rolf's tenure as the Duke of Normandy:

The son of [Rolf the Ganga] was William, the father of Richard, the father of the second Richard, the father of Robert Longspear, the father of William the Bastard, king of England. From him all later kings of England are descended. (Chapter 24. Ganger-Hrólf Is Outlawed)

The Heimskringla was written in about 1230. Yet, this statement remains true to this day. Rolf's descendant was William the Bastard, later known as William the Conqueror. And William the Conqueror's descendants included the House of Windsor. As of this writing, one of their sons, Charles, still sits on the throne of England, over eleven centuries later.

The Rise and Fall of Viking Ireland

To the west of England is Ireland. The relatively small island sat at the edge of Christian civilization until the 9th century, and was comparable to Scandinavia in other ways as well. If one traveled north into Scandinavia, eventually one would pass hostile terrain and into the dark north, where one could easily fall prey to the hostile natives, supernatural monsters, or the elements of the dark and cold. If one traveled west to the ends of Ireland, one could easily be killed by the hostile natives, supernatural monsters, or the elements of the endless ocean.

It is probably this remote location and its lack of direct involvement in the Roman world to the south that made Ireland an attractive location. The Roman-educated St. Patrick began the island's conversion to Christianity in the fifth century, well before the Vikings set sail.

These Celts, operating largely on their own at the edge of the known world, developed a unique institution of Christianity, known to scholars today as "Insular Christianity." It had intimate contact with the Roman Church, but played largely by its own rules until the 664 Synod of Whitby, which held up Roman orthodoxy over Celtic tradition, and required the Celtic church to submit to Roman authority or face spiritual repercussions.

By the time of the Synod, Ireland had already done much to "save" Christian civilization. It was in Ireland that the art of the illuminated manuscript was practiced, developed, and perfected—those items that held mysterious secrets the Vikings didn't care much about, but were decorated with precious metals and stones. And later the Vikings would learn that the interiors of the books were just as valuable as their outsides. But that was still years away.

The Heimskringla records various raids against Ireland, though their historicity and chronology is disputed (Sturluson, n.d., Chapter 33. King Harald Partitions the Realm among His Sons). The first reliable reports of longships visiting Ireland date from as early as 795 (Parker, 2015. Chronology). At the time the Vikings had arrived, there were several "High

Kings" in Ireland, but they were small political powers, and it was the monasteries that still held much of the political influence and, most important for the Vikings, the wealth.

In 795 the Vikings raided the monastery of Iona, an island off the west coast of Scotland. This attack, to the Ionans, seemed to come from nowhere, and these pagan raiders seemed not less than demons (Parker, 2015. Chapter 1). Refugee monks fled to Ireland, many of them contributing to the Abbey of Kells in the central-west of the island (Cahill, 1996. Is there any hope?). To protect precious items from these raids, Irish monks began to bury sacred items for safe keeping. This is how the beloved Book of Kells, visible today at Trinity College in Dublin, was protected, jewels, gold, and text, from the raiders. As Cahill writes,

In modern times, and still today, a farmer's spade will occasionally uncover some lost treasure, like the Ardagh Chalice; or some noble family, reduced even to peasant status by Ireland's subsequent woeful history, will be found to have preserved through all the centuries a weathered codex as fantastic as the Cathach of Columcille. (ibid.)

But this pattern should be recognizable to the reader by now. The Vikings soon evolved from desiring precious stones and metals from their targets, to desiring a kingdom of their own.

In 837 Thorgest, "the Sea-King," smelled blood in the water as a war between the High Kings of Tara and Munster broke out and he saw promise in the chaos (Extra Credits, 2018g). Within only a few years after setting out, in 840–1, the Vikings were noted to still be on the island. The Annals of Ulster note that the heathens were "still at Dublin," noting that they did not seem to be on the island for solely a smash-and-grab operation (Parker, 2015. Chapter 2).

Thorgest, an Odin-worshiping heathen, had no intention of ever converting to Christianity. He sacked the Abbey in Armagh and declared himself the new Abbot. This gave him the right to collect the monastery's rent from the survivors (Extra Credits, 2018g). Of course, this title, which doubtless meant little to him, only whetted his appetite.

Viking ambitions over the Emerald Isle pervaded Viking thought in the region for decades. Dublin's location was not accidental. It was chosen for its port proximity across the Irish Sea, where Norse forces in Ireland could link up with the Great Heathen Army and its descendant kingdoms in Britain (Parker, 2015.

Chapter 2). Dublin was a prosperous Viking port city. Ireland not only had a favorable climate to much of Scandinavia, but was at the center of the Viking trade network. Ships regularly visited Dublin on their way south toward the Mediterranean, and back on the return trip to Scandinavia. Many Vikings, however, chose to stay in Ireland and make it their home, despite the conquest of a Norse Irish Kingdom being an ongoing project. The Vikings brought an althing (i.e. a ruling council) to Dublin, which had a thriving artisanal quarter, and had begun to intermingle with the locals (ibid.). A generation of mixed Irish-Norse was growing up in and around Dublin, and was leaving the port city and leading lives of their own (Extra Credits, 2018g). Not only that, but the political project—partly because the Danelaw prevented a combined Norse Irish Sea Empire from reinforcing them, and partly because trade and commerce had become more profitable than wars and raids—was more or less on hold.

Though they looked different, practiced a different religion, and spoke and wrote in a strange language, the Norse had simply become another faction fighting for control of the High Kingship of Ireland. One among many. A string of Irish victories in 848 convinced the Norse to ally with some local Irish factions, and this essentially doomed the project from taking root ever again, now that the Irish knew they could use the Norse as much as the Norse could use them.

These events culminated in the Battle of Tara in 980 and the Battle of Clontarf in 1014. At Tara, the Vikings were decisively defeated and the King of Dublin was forced to, ironically, flee to a monastery (Extra Credits, 2018g). The "red-slaughter" at Tara was followed by the siege and capture of Dublin by native Irish forces. With the complete slaughter and rout of his forces, the King of Dublin gave up his title, converted to Christianity, and fled to Iona to live out his days as a monk (Parker, 2015. Chapter 10).

The 1014 Battle of Clontarf is usually used as the traditional "end" of Viking rule or influence in the Irish national story. At Clontarf, King Brian Boru, whose harp adorns some versions of the traditional Irish flag, decisively defeated the Vikings in battle and drove them from his island, just as St. Patrick drove out the snakes, or King Alfred the Great and Emperor Charlemagne drove out the Danes and Saxons, respectively, from their realms (ibid.). After the battle was won, King Brian went to his tent to pray, when a vengeant Viking crept into his tent and axed him in the back (Extra Credits, 2018g).

Though this tale is important for the national story of Ireland, it greatly stretches the truth. By the eleventh century,

With Dublin captured, the Irish Vikings ceased to be significant political players, exercising at best a partial autonomy from their increasingly powerful Irish neighbors. The Norsemen found themselves caught up in domestic Irish struggles, operating as the client of one side or another in the tussle between Máel Sechnaill and the growing power of Brian Bóruma (or Boru). (Parker, 2015. Chapter 10).

Basically, King Brian Boru was perfectly willing to use the Norse to his own ends. Even this division between Norse and Irish is oversimplified. As mentioned above, whole generations had grown up that were at least part Norse and part Irish. Many of the men in Boru's army were mixed-race, spoke both languages, and could claim heritage from both sides of the conflict—as could many who fought on the other side at Clontarf.

Still, it is an important tale to Irish heritage and cultural identity. The Vikings represented a threat from over the sea, and the terrifying image of villains without language or culture—as they would seem to frightened monks who did not speak their language and were not given the time to ask where the Vikings came from or what they wanted—endures for a reason. Not only in national myths, but in popular culture as well.

Thomas Cahill's How the Irish Saved Civilization is a fantastic and well-researched book; however, he finds it difficult to hide his contempt for the Viking attacks on Ireland. This is understandable, as the Vikings came seeking plunder and conquest, and anger at that kind of wanton destruction is a perfectly reasonable reaction to have. He writes,

> Ireland was under siege. The Viking terrorists had discovered its peaceful monasteries, now rich in precious objects. The monks built round towers without ground-floor entrances and hauled their plate up rope ladders, which they then pulled up after themselves. But such towers were no match for Vikings, nor were the monks, by this time growing sleek and tame. Nor apparently were the warriors, many of whom had turned into relatively peaceful, even erudite, laymen. The illiterate Vikings often destroyed books by ripping off bejeweled covers for booty. (Cahill, 1996. Is there any hope?)

The Vikings were not, strictly speaking, an illiterate culture. They had their own runic alphabet which is still visible in examples of standing stones all across northern Europe. But they did at first, as is represented in most clashing cultures, struggle to understand the importance of the inside of the illuminated manuscripts. But in the process of Norse-Irish interaction, the Norse who chose to stay in Ireland had more-or-less become Irishized. This is clearly visible above, with the invasion of Ireland beginning with a Viking "Sea-King" naming himself Abbot of a monastery and remaining pagan, but ending with the King of Dublin fleeing to Iona to be a Christian monk.

Though the Viking dream of a Norse Kingdom on the island was never realized, as it was in Normandy and in England, they left several non-genetic legacies in their wake. The first was Dublin, whose importance as a port city at the nexus of the North Sea-Mediterranean Trade only continued to grow as time went on. It also became the first part of the island to fall to future invaders (these ones not Vikings, but their descendants: Normans) and serve as the base of operations for English invasion.

The dark side to this legacy, of both Viking political rule and their economic influence over the island, was the reintroduction of slavery (Extra Credits, 2018g). Nordic culture tolerated slavery, and indeed engaged in slavery as far as Africa and Iceland. By some reports, slavery (called thralldom in Norse languages) survived in parts of Scandinavia as late as the 1100s, and by at least one report, as late as the 1400s, in isolated pockets of Sweden (Parker, 2015. Notes: Chapter 1. n.31). In Ireland, however, slavery was banned by St. Patrick, who saw it as sinful.

But in the Patrician exchange, Ireland, lacking the power and implacable traditions of Rome, had been received into Christianity, which transformed Ireland into Something New, something never seen before—a Christian culture, where slavery and human sacrifice became unthinkable, and warfare, though impossible for humans to eradicate, diminished markedly. (Cahill, 1996. How the Irish Saved Civilization).

But while the Norse never achieved dominion over the entirety of the island, they were the economic powerhouse, as shown by the astronomical rise of Dublin over the island's industry. And while Vikings captured native Irish and sold them as slaves in al-Andalus and Iceland, their mixed descendants saw less and less of a problem with the practice, which continued in Ireland until the Normans, who were so Christian many would set off to spread their religion by conquest in the Crusades, progressively re-banished the practice as they chopped and sliced their way through the island in the succeeding centuries (Rodgers, 2009. p. 20).

On Iceland

Shortly after the world was made, God came to visit Adam and Eve. They happily received their Creator and showed him everything they had in their house, including their children. However, Eve had not finished washing her children, and when God saw the ones she presented to him, he knew that there were some missing.

"Where are your other children?" God asked.

Eve responded that this was all of them.

But God, being omnipotent, knew that there were others she had hidden. "What man hides from God," he said, "God will hide from man." And he turned those children invisible.

These invisible children of Eve took their abode in the mounds, hills, and rocks of Iceland. Their descendants became the elves, and only by their desire do they become visible to the descendants of Adam and Eve's other children (Árnason, 1866. pp. 19-20).

As mentioned in the previous chapter, Iceland was devoid of human habitation entirely until at least the 6th century. It had never boasted a great civilization like Rome, or even the decentralized societies of Scandinavia. And it was certainly not the birthplace of humanity, as the above story implied. Yet the story of the huldufólk, the "hidden people," is a story rooted in Norse mythology of the elves, later baptized by Christianity, and is still in effect to this day, as modern stories of elves and hidden people living in the rocks and land are still commonplace. For example, in 2013, proposed road construction was halted in an Icelandic suburb because elf-rights groups allied with environmentalists protested the construction.

The Papar, if they did indeed discover and make their homeland on the island soon to be named Iceland, did not leave a lasting cultural or societal legacy on the island. That would be left up to the Norse. Likely sailing northwards from the Faroe Islands, the island was, according to the Sagas, first discovered by a man named Floki, who followed the "trail" of a raven he let loose that did not return (a dubious, albeit common method of finding land in pre-navigational days). The "trail" led him to Iceland, which he found to have a pleasant summer, but a harsh and forbidding winter. He returned home to Scandinavia to report on the land that reminded him of Niflheim, christening it Iceland.

Floki, so called "Raven Floki" for his method of discovery, set out on his first voyage to Iceland in 868. In the years that followed, wealthy and powerful Scandinavian lords would start to gather power about themselves and place crowns on their own heads, modeling their kingdoms not after the adventurous trading confederations of their homeland, but after the growing feudal monarchies of Christendom. To many Norse, accustomed to an adventurous free spirit, this was unacceptable. Scandinavia was becoming too crowded, and its politics too authoritarian.

Unlike the rest of Europe, Iceland had no natives—minus huldufólk—and so if one wanted to sail to Iceland, and was willing to build a home, farm the fields, and fish the waters, they were more than able to do so. And all without having to worry about angry, armed locals!

And so Iceland became populated.

Two of these most famous settlers were Ingolf Arnasson and his foster-brother Hjorleif. On their second expedition, they arrived on the western coast of Iceland with the intention of settling there. Ingold brought along two pillars from the high seat of his home farm in Norway. According to pagan practice, Ingolf cast the pillars into the sea as soon as he was in sight of the Icelandic shore, and swore to build his farm wherever they were found. At first they couldn't find them, but after some time and searching, the brothers came across the pillars washed up in a sheltered harbor filled with steam from local hot springs. They named their settlement "Smoky Bay," in Norse, Reykjavik (Parker, 2015. Chapter 4).

Iceland soon exploded in population (compared to its previous population of zero). Vikings made the island their home and raided the British Isles without needing to concern themselves with the share they owed to the Kings and Lords of their ancestral homelands. This also meant the Vikings brought thralldom, i.e. slavery, to Iceland. Akhil Bakshi, writing of his travels in Iceland in 2012, was told that, "Any Icelander can tell you which village in Norway his family originated from 1,000 years ago, or the Irish or Scottish village from which his ancestress was abducted by the Vikings" (Bakshi, 2012).

Today Iceland is far from an overcrowded country. But only after a short time, Iceland had outgrown its sort of anarchic existence. It had developed into a country that needed, if not a form of organization, some way of solving disputes and arguments among themselves. The solution the Icelanders came up with was the Althing. Norse communities used Things, i.e. councils, to manage day-to-day governance of their communities for ages. The Althing was exactly what it sounded like: the dominant council that governed the entire island.

Around the turn of the millennium, the Vikings were increasingly Christianized. Major Viking lords had converted and settled in the British Isles, Continental Europe, and even the Scandinavian homeland. Iceland was pressured to convert by all of their trading partners, so the Althing convened to discuss whether Iceland would follow the ways of the old gods or bow to this new one. Arguments were heard on both sides, but the Christian contingent was clearly louder. The judge who presided over the Althing, however, was an avowed Pagan. After listening to the arguments, he agreed: Iceland should become Christian.

However. Anyone who refused to accept the new god should be allowed to worship privately however they saw fit, and not be bothered.

And so Iceland took a step closer to

becoming an integral part of the European world.

Yet even at this far edge of the world, things seemed to be getting too crowded for some of the Vikings. They sought greener pastures.

Of Greenland and Vinland

To the northeast of Iceland, less than 400 miles (643.7 km) away, is Greenland. This, of course, is where Greenland, the world's largest island, comes the closest to Iceland. A mere four days' sail (in favorable conditions) isn't particularly inspiring, considering that 80% of the confusingly-named Greenland was covered in ice.

There are many early stories of lands that seem to be in the general direction of Greenland compared to the rest of the Nordic world, but none of them are able to be confirmed. What's more is context clues point to other explanations: as-yet-unidentified communities far closer to Scandinavia, and simple mirages on the ocean surface (Parker, 2015. Chapter 5).

In 970, Thorvald Asvaldsson fled Norway with his son Erik (later known as "the Red") to escape punishment for manslaughter (Sturluson, n.d. Chapter 86. Leif Eiríksson Joins the King's Court). They went where all Vikings fleeing the authoritarian grip of the law usually went: Iceland. Though Thorvald and Erik were latecomers to Icelandic settlement and most of the good land was already taken, they found some harsh terrain in the western part of the island that had not-particularly-decent soil, and even harsher weather. They built their home out of driftwood, and it is likely this need for lumber that drove Icelanders to venture westwards (Extra Credits, 2018i).

One day, a pair of Erik's servants accidentally caused a rockslide that destroyed a neighbor's home. This incident led to an argument and Erik killed two of his neighbor's servants in the process. Iceland was still run by the Althing, and had a pretty anarchic sense of how a man might defend his home and honor, but Erik was clearly headed for disciplinary action. He elected to try his hand somewhere else. As Parker writes, "Exactly what point he first reached along Greenland's eastern coast is uncertain, but it will not have been an inviting landscape that greeted him," (Chapter 5). Erik and his household spent some time looking for whatever the island's Reykjavik would be, and came upon a place he called Hvarf. This unconfirmed location became the center of Erik's Norse settlement (ibid.).

When Erik returned to Iceland, it was with a longboat full of bear skins, seal hides, and walrus ivory and the enticing name of a new land: "Greenland." The name evoked images of lush, fertile fields, and enticed a number of settlers who longed for a similar freedom in a land unburdened by the Althing's authority. In 986, 25 ships laden with settlers set out for Greenland (ibid.).

This was a prelude. Erik's son Leif would soon have his own personal conflict with neighbors on Greenland, and decided to follow in his father's footsteps and sail further west. The land he found was more fertile and green than either Greenland or Iceland. It was apparently filled with grapes, which led to Leif christening the country "Vinland" (Parker, 2015. Chapter 6).

Unlike Iceland and most of Greenland, however, Vinland was populated. Historians are still not certain exactly which tribes the Vikings encountered on the island that would later be named Newfoundland, but the Vikings called them Skraelings (Harper, n.d.c). The Skraelings (with respect to the unknown name they called themselves), at least according to the Norse Sagas, seemed fine at first with allowing the

Vikings to settle.

After some time, they were even interested in trading with the Norse. The Skraelings wanted Viking steel (Parker, 2015. Chapter 6). The entirety of the Americas, from Vinland to Alaska to Tierra del Fuego, would be devoid of steel until the Spanish brought it (again) in the 1500s. But the Vikings (who were very far from the nearest forge) weren't willing to give up their steel.

What they did have to offer the Skraelings was butter. The Skraelings accepted the trade... but there weren't any domesticated milking animals north of the Andes, and the sudden introduction of lactose into their systems made the Skraelings deeply sick (Extra Credits, 2018j). These misunderstandings led Skraeling attacks to increase, and according to Parker (2015),

Although the skraelings were beaten off and their chieftain killed, Karlsefni [the Viking chieftain] realized that, few as they were, the Vikings could not resist such attacks indefinitely. After staying a further winter— which the impossibility of sailing back home through the winter ice constrained them to do— he ordered the colony abandoned and a return to Greenland. (Chapter 6)

The hostility of the Skraelings made for a dramatic tale in the Sagas, and certainly discouraged further colonization. However, the land was still precious, in particular for its abundant lumber compared to timber-sparse Greenland (ibid.). The Sagas end with victory over the Skraelings, but we know from archaeological evidence at the site near L'Anse aux Meadows that the colony persisted, likely as a seasonal spot for Norse lumberjacks (Parker, 2015. Chapter 5).

As the Greenland colony declined and Iceland stabilized (and became further entwined in the Scandinavian trade network) Vinland and its northern neighbor, Markland, declined in popularity. The Viking colony, as a non-seasonal settlement, seems to have been completely abandoned by the 1100s. An Icelandic bishop, Erik Gnuppson, sailed westwards to Vinland in 1121, and nothing more was heard of him (Parker, 2015. Chapter 6). After this the lands passed into the murky realm of mythology with the writing of the Saga of Erik the Red, composed in the 1200s, and the Saga of the Greenlanders in the 1300s) (ibid.).

Greenland, like Iceland, accepted direct rule from the Norwegian King in 1261 (Parker, 2015. Chapter 5). In 1341, the Western Settlement on

Greenland was abandoned, and reportedly captured by Skraelings (who almost certainly were not the same group of peoples that the Norse encountered in Vinland) (Parker, 2015. Chronology). It is reported in 1379 that attacks from the Skraelings increased in Greenland, and by then royal interest in maintaining the colony had declined, but it continued on as a vestigial realm of the Norwegian Empire for another three-quarters of a century. The story quickly gets lost in the dark pages of history. For example, Parker (2015) writes,

As to the date of the colony's disappearance, the testimony of the Hvalsey wedding suggests that Viking Greenland was still a fully functioning community in 1408, while the archaeological evidence from Herjolfsnes indicates that it continued in this way at least to some point between 1425 and 1450. Anecdotal reports hint at some kind of attack in 1418, with further assaults in the period after 1420, but thereafter it is hard to be conclusive (Chapter 5).

In 1448, Pope Nicholas V ordered a Bishop in Iceland to send a priest to Greenland, though no expedition was sent out (ibid.). There is no official date for the disestablishment of the Greenland colonies, nor a death date for the last Viking to fall to Skraeling spears, but by 1475, the Norse colonial experiment in Greenland was very much over.

The Norse journeys to North America are undoubtedly one of their least significant contributions to the social, cultural, economic, political, and even religious and genetic influences on the world—yet they are still some of the most interesting and well-regarded. When discussing the Columbian Exchange, when Spanish and Portuguese ships crossed the Atlantic to "discover" the Western Hemisphere and begin the colonial period, it is almost always marked with an asterisk to indicate that they were not the first Europeans to visit the Americas; that it was the Vikings who made it there first.

Why the Viking colonial experiments in Vinland, Greenland, and (to a lesser extent) Markland failed are still the subject of analysis. For our purposes, we have to simply conclude that the European Empires, and the Vikings themselves, were not at the social, political, economic, or even technological point to conduct long-term colonial projects.

That said, we must now turn to the Viking projects that did succeed. Namely, their colonization and conquest of Europe.

CHAPTER 3
THE CHRISTIAN VIKINGS AND THEIR SUCCESSORS

The Norse had more in common with their Christian neighbors than they initially thought. For example, the Norse had a god who was nailed to a tree as a form of human sacrifice (Odin), as did the Christians (Jesus). The Christians were also counting on the return of Christ and the end of the world, which they saw in the last book of the Bible, called Revelations. The Norse had their own version of this they called Ragnarok.

Ragnarok was referred to as "the destiny of the gods." It was predicted to begin with the Fimbulwinter, the "Mighty," "Terrible," or (occasionally) the "Strange Winter," that was said to last three years. After this, humanity would completely break down: Fratricide and oathbreaking would become commonplace, the wolves would leave the forest to devour children at play, and Midgard would fall into complete ruin.

At last, the gods would emerge from Asgard and Vanaheim to fight the giants emerging from Niflheim and Muspellheim. The Dwarves and Elves would leave secret places and join the fight. The ship made of nails, Naglfar, will carry the jotuns out of their realm and to the battle. Fenrir, the wolf chained into place by moonlight, would break free and eat the sun, plunging the world into darkness.

It was Odin himself who would spear Fenrir. But the battle would be his last, and the King of the Gods would die by the wolf's teeth. One of Odin's sons would avenge his father, but the victory would be short-lived. Freyr would fight Surtr, and die by fire. Thor would fight the world serpent with his mighty hammer Mjolnir, but it would all be for naught. After this, the earth would sink into the sea, and the stars would go dark.

The Vikings believed they were living through the Fimbulwinter. Though it was only supposed to last three years, this was more for the poetry than anything else (Orchard, 1998); the winter was "strange," after all. It is possible that crop failures in Scandinavia contributed to the Norse thinking that they were living in the end times (Gunn, 2000). It may have also been an important factor in the first raids across the North and Baltic Seas. As the raiders fueled chaos and disorder wherever they went, establishing trading outposts, forts, and entire kingdoms, more chaos and disorder resulted, further contributing to this idea that the end was nigh for the Christians as well.

As for the Norse pagan religion, their world really was ending. As the Vikings established polities as far west as North America, as far south as Normandy, and as far east as Russia, they were Christianized bit by bit. As mentioned in the previous chapter, as the Viking wars of conquest ground to a halt, both political and economic pressure pushed the descendants of the original state-building projects to adopt Christianity. The Vikings who maintained the tiny city-state of Dublin were born mostly of Irish women, and raised Catholic. The raiders who accompanied Rolf the Ganga and settled Normandy, by the turn of the millennium, gave rise to a generation of French-speaking Catholic Normans. The Great Heathen Army settled Britain, and gave rise to a series of small Norse-settled kingdoms. Iceland was convinced to turn Christian, with respect to Norse pagans and their traditions.

And, as we shall see, this development was not limited to the Norse liminal spaces. The Norse homelands of Denmark, Norway, and Sweden were soon to convert to Christianity, and the rest of their kingdoms with them. The Vikings conquered large swaths of Europe and changed basically everything about it, and in the process, Europe changed almost everything about the Vikings.

The Rise of Rus'

While the Norwegians and Danes were raiding monasteries and carving out kKingdoms in the North Sea and the western world, the Swedes did the same across the Baltic (Parker, 2015. Chapter 7). Eastern Europe, between the Baltic and Black Seas has been, until relatively recently, a mix of swamplands and grassy steppe, where nomadic tribes of central Asia met forest-dwelling peoples in the wet marshlands that surrounded the Danube, Dniester, Dnieper, Don, and the Volga, the longest rivers in Europe.

Most of these rivers and their tributaries criss-crossed through lands ruled by Slavic-speaking peoples. None of them, of course, fully bisected the continent, so it became necessary to build trading posts where Vikings could change vessels and go from one river to another, carrying their loot on the way back (Richards, 2005. Chapter 6). Initially these loots were small, perhaps driven by the reward at the other end of the earth: the great, prosperous, and mighty city of Constantinople.

Constantinople, today's Istanbul, was built during the Roman era as an eastern counterpart to Rome itself. Originally named after the Emperor Constantine, sat at the edge of Europe, on a small peninsula facing Asia across the Bosporus Strait, the Black Sea to the north, and the Sea of Marmara to the south, feeding into the Mediterranean. Constantinople, centuries after Rome fell to Gothic kings, was sustained by the forces of trade. The capital of the Byzantine Empire was the perfect vantage point to serve as a marketplace of trade from both east (Asia) and west (Europe), and north (the Black Sea) and south (the Mediterranean) (Parker, 2015. Chapter 7).

The walls that the Turks brought down with cannonfire in 1453 were the very same walls that must have amazed and inspired the Vikings who sighted it in the ninth and tenth centuries (Extra Credits, 2018h). And they were the walls that assured the Byzantines that the Vikings would not stand a chance to sack it, but they could camp outside and starve the city of its precious trade. This made the incredibly wealthy city a tempting—very tempting—target for Danegeld (Parker, 2015. Chapter 7).

But it was not the only final destination for eastward facing Vikings. Sailing south down the Volga led the longships eventually to the Caspian Sea. The Sea opened the Norse to the trade of the Middle East: All the wealth of Persia, Transoxiana, and the Arab Caliphates were open to them (Richards, 2005. Chapter 6). Vikings were seen as far as Baghdad (though usually not for any raiding purposes; that was far too far for the raiders, but Baghdad was a rich market and a place where the most ambitious Norse merchants could buy and sell) (Parker, 2015. Chapter 7).

As the saying goes, however, it was about the journey, not the destination. For while Constantinople and Baghdad were certainly influential and important points in Viking history, the real lasting effect the Vikings had on the region were in the trade posts they established between the Baltic, Black, and Caspian Seas, and the legacy they left behind.

Over the years these trading posts grew into forts, and the forts into towns, and finally into cities that became kingdoms. One of the most powerful and famous of these city-states that erected a kingdom around it was Kyiv, and the kingdom that developed around it is known to historians as Kyivan Rus' (ibid.). The "Rus" here is, of course, where we get the word "Russia" from, but its origins come from the Vikings. Though the exact nature of the name "Rus" is not entirely clear, all theories point to it referencing the Vikings, not the locals. The most prevalent theory is that "rus" comes from a Uralic language (which would have been prominent in the region at the time) and referred to the "men who row" (Harper, n.d.d).

Just as the Vikings sent mostly men across Europe to raid, pillage, and conquer, and those Vikings married local women to birth a generation of part-Norse, part-Irish/French/etc. people, these eastern Vikings did the same with Slavic women who settled near their trading posts (Parker, 2015. Chapter 7). As the years went on and the kingdoms grew, they were increasingly populated by part-Norse, part-Slavic people, who drew from the political and militant tradition of their fathers' Viking heritage, and the religious, social, and linguistic tradition of their Slavic mothers (Extra Credits, 2018h).

One of the most influential of these mixed-race easterners was a woman named Olga. Olga was married to Igor, the Prince of Kyiv, and the son of Rurik, who founded the Kingdom of Kyivan Rus' by uniting the various city-states under Norse control.

Prince Igor was not as capable of a ruler as his father was, or even as his wife would soon prove to be. The Kyivans had a complex relationship with a nearby tribe known as the Drevelians. They were sometimes allies in the raiding of Byzantine towns and outposts, and sometimes they were enemies for influence, loot, or territory in the region. Sometime in 945, Igor demanded tribute from the Drevelians. The tribes paid, but on his return to Kyiv, Igor decided that it wasn't enough, so he turned back to demand more, at which point the Drevelians murdered him (Parker, 2015. Chapter 7).

Igor and Olga's son, Sviatoslav, was still a child, and so Olga took up the regency. But she now had to immediately prosecute a war. Knowing that they could easily be overwhelmed by the Drevelians, Olga chose a method reflective of the traditional Viking crossroads of brutality and trickery. The Drevelian leader who murdered Prince Igor demanded that Olga marry him. Olga said she needed to consider the offer, but would let her "honored guests" sleep in their ships. The Drevelians agreed, and the

Kyivan people carried the Drevelians towards their ships. At first the Drevelians considered this a great honor, but soon it was revealed that they were not being taken to their ships, but to a trench dug the night before, where they were buried alive (Extra Credits, 2018h).

Olga later sent an offer of further negotiations to the Drevelians, requesting that she visit her husband's grave in their territory. When she arrived, she required a great quantity of mead for a funeral feast. The Drevelians, seeing as she was weeping (and therefore was honest about her intention to mourn her husband), supplied the alcohol, and then proceeded to get drunk. While the enemy was too drunk to defend themselves, Olga ordered her men to slaughter them one by one. By the Byzantine account of that evening, some 5,000 Drevelians were killed on Olga's orders that night (Galeotti, 2021. Chapter 1).

Much of Olga's career reflects this power dynamic. She was often underestimated (possibly because of her gender), only to respond to her foes with a mix of trickery and brutality, oft found in the tales her ancestors told about Loki, Thor, and Odin.

But this conflict with the Drevelians was not a sustainable one. It may have worked out in her favor this time around, but Olga realized that she needed powerful allies to be able to maintain her and her son's position. In 950, she sailed to Constantinople and converted to Christianity (ibid.). Priests of Greek rites were soon sailing northwards to baptize large swaths of the population of Kyivan Rus'. For her efforts, Olga was baptized with the name "Elena" and made a Saint in the Orthodox Church (Lewis, 2019). She was even blessed with the title "Equal to the Apostles." It is usually here that the history of the Vikings in Ukraine and Russia slips into a more general history of Ukraine and Russia, and the Vikings feature increasingly less.

The Last Vikings

The Vikings were known as fearsome warriors far from their homeland and long after the last Viking fought their last battle. And as we saw in France and Ireland, local Christian kings were eager to turn the Vikings as a weapon onto their enemies. The Roman Emperors residing in Constantinople came to the same conclusion—that they could hire Vikings as their own personal elite soldiers, rather than pay them simply to leave them alone. These men became known as the Varangian Guard (Norwich, 1998. Introduction).

The Varangians were not only a highly

honored position in Byzantine society, but became a badge of honor for returning Varangians to the Viking homeland (Parker, 2015. Chapter 9). Varangians fought in almost all of the Byzantine's Empire's major battles, from the tenth century well into the fifteenth (Norwich, 2003. Chapter 9). Norse royalty even sent their princes to fight in the Varangian Guard.

One of these princes eventually rose to become the King of Norway. Harald Sigurdsson, known as the Hardrada, the "Hard Ruler," served in the Varangian Guard before returning to Norway to serve as King Harald III for twenty years (Parker, 2015. Chapter 9). A descendant of King Knut "the Holy," Harald, a Catholic, also had a claim on the Kingdom of England, or at least the lands once declared the "Danelaw." The dream of reestablishing a North Sea Empire occupied the minds of Norwegian and Danish lawmakers ever since it fell apart into different kingdoms. When King Edward the Confessor died in January 1066, Harald seized his chance and invaded England (McLynn, 1998. Chapter 9).

King Edward the Confessor was the direct descendant of Alfred the Great, the King of Wessex who fought Guthram to a standstill and convinced him to convert to Christianity (Howarth, 1986. Introduction). He unfortunately left his succession open by flirting with passing the throne to his cousin Svend II, the King of Denmark, or possibly passing it on to King Harald in Norway, both of them descendants of Knut the Holy. And across the English Channel was the direct descendant of Rolf the Ganga, Duke William, then known as "William the Bastard."

Yet it was notable that none of these men lived in England. The Witenagemot, the Anglo-Saxon precursor to a modern parliament (more akin to the Nordic kingsmoot, a meeting of nobles to decide who shall succeed to the throne) decided in favor of King Edward's brother-in-law, Harold Godwinson (ibid.). The vaguely Nordic patronym, and Harold's own (distant) descent from Knut the Holy only served to highlight the truth of the matter: Whoever won, the next King of England would be a descendant of the Vikings.

Harald Hardrada set sail from Norway and invaded England from the north. King Harold called his banners and summoned every man who could lift a sword to his kingdom's defense. The result was the Battle of Stamford Bridge, just outside the city of York, taking place on the

25th of September, 1066. In the battle, the Hardrada was killed with an arrow to his throat (Parker, 2015. Chapter 9). Their king's death ended the Norwegian threat to the conquest of England, and the last, greatest hope for resurrecting the North Sea Empire. But the path to Harold Godwinson's throne was not yet secure. Immediately after defeating the Norwegians, he had to turn his army south to face a Viking of a different sort.

William, "the Bastard," was just a Duke in Normandy. After being legitimized, he inherited the Dukedom from his father Robert. Robert's aunt, Emma, had married King Aethelred "the Unready," King of England, when he took refuge in Normandy during a Viking raid. And it was through the connection to his grandaunt, along with his close relationship with and blessing of the Pope, that William claimed the English throne after King Edward's death (McLynn, 1998. Chapter 5).

William and his Normans landed on the coast of England, and on October 14, 1066, William's Norman knights met Harold's Anglo-Saxon huscarls in battle. Harold was hit in the eye with an arrow and killed, and Duke William the Bastard became King William the Conqueror (Bridgeford, 2009. Chapter 9).

William spent the entirety of the rest of his reign consolidating rule over England, putting down rebellions from across the island as he sought to deprive Anglo-Saxon lords of their lands and titles to reward his loyal knights and attendants. Descendants of the Norman Kings, begun by William the Conqueror, still sit the throne of England to this day. William's dynasty, though it has changed names, hands, and even nationalities multiple times over the last nine-and-a-half centuries, has never been removed from power, as the Anglo-Saxon and Danish kings were.

There was never a point where the Viking Age decisively ended. There was no peace treaty from the King of the Vikings signed with the Pope, or some Dissolution of All Viking Raids declared in an Althing with all Viking lords in attendance. It was more of a gradual dissolution that was difficult to pinpoint, partly because the Vikings had been assimilated into European culture and customs, and the Europeans, in turn, had themselves become assimilated into the Viking world.

The Normans are, as literal Christian descendants of the Vikings who ravaged Europe for centuries, possibly the best example, and single most powerful force in the post-Viking era, to show this. Another Kingdom that the Normans set up and conquered was about as far and as different from Scandinavia as could be: Sicily and southern Italy (see Brown, 2003).

The dynasty, the House of de Hauteville, became the Kings of Sicily after raiding and conquering their way through the Mediterranean. They were never truly at peace, and spent a great deal of time trying to conquer the Byzantine Empire and seat one of their own on the ancient throne of the Eastern Roman Empire. All of it was recorded by the Emperor's daughter Anna Komnene, in a record historians refer to as The Alexiad.

Though the Normans failed to conquer Constantinople, their attack vastly depleted the Empire's resources. A few years later, when the Turks defeated a Byzantine garrison at the Battle of Manzikert in 1071, it signaled to Emperor Alexios Komnenos, whom The Alexiad is named after, that he needed help if he was going to continue to defend the gates of Christendom from the Saracen (i.e. Islamic) menace any longer.

He sent a message to the Pope asking for aid. The result was the Crusades. Pope Urban II called for all good Christian knights to assemble and march to the Holy Land to retake it from the infidel (Asbridge, 2009. Chapter 1). This was far more than what Emperor Alexios had in mind, but what he needed was soldiers and weapons, and at that point he was willing to take what he could get. Of course, not everyone came out of religious piety and zeal, and ironically, one of the most powerful contingents of the initial crusading force was Bohemond of Taranto, the son of the de Hauteville leader who sought to seat himself on the throne in Constantinople. And with him were thousands of Norman knights who couldn't break into the capital of the Byzantine Empire years earlier, but this time were invited in to defend the lands on the other side.

They were Vikings of a very different sort, indeed.

This is not a history of the crusades, so at this point we will leave the crusaders behind. But it is notable that Bohemond, like many of his fellow crusaders, broke his oath to return all captured lands to Byzantine control. He seized Antioch for himself, and crowned himself Prince in 1098 (Brown, 2003. Chapter XXI).

The Life, Art, and Death of Snorri Sturluson

By the 12th Century, the Viking Age was very much over. Normans controlled Antioch as a minor princedom of their own. The Kingdom of Jerusalem (roughly the same borders as modern Israel) was under siege from the great Sultan of Egypt, Saladin. The Byzantine Empire was none-too-happy about the breaking of oath, but was probably happy not to have to worry about Danegeld. The descendants of William the Conqueror had moved on from consolidating their rule in England to conquering both Ireland and France, and in Iceland Christianity had advanced.

Enter Snorri Sturluson.

He was born in Iceland as a member of the powerful Sturlungar clan in 1179. As a result of a violent incident, in which Snorri's father was attacked by the wife of a priest, who threatened to stab him in the eye, "to make him like his hero, Odin," Snorri was raised from a young age by Jon Loftsson, a relative of Norwegian royalty. This led to Snorri receiving an excellent education and forging connections in high places, at the expense of never seeing his parents ever again. His father died in 1183, and his mother later squandered Snorri's share of the inheritance. Jon Loftsson, Snorri's benefactor, died in 1197. From Snorri's father-in-law, he inherited a rich estate and a chieftainship.

Snorri was soon known as a poet and a lawyer. In 1215, he became lawspeaker of the Althing. In 1218, he was invited to Norway by the king, and left the lawspeaker position to travel across the sea to the continent. In Norway he became acquainted with the young King Haakon IV. The king and his court showered gifts upon him, and in return, Snorri wrote poetry about them.

Snorri was mainly interested in history and culture. The Norwegians, however, had political aspirations in Iceland. King Haakon sought to extend his rule across the sea. He made Snorri a "skutilsvein" (a title roughly equivalent to a knight) and made Snorri declare an oath of loyalty. In theory, Norwegian rule could extend to Iceland without a war of conquest, merely provided a majority of the Althing passed a resolution to bring royal rule to their island. By befriending Snorri, King Haakon had cultivated a powerful and key member of the council that ruled the island.

Snorri returned to Iceland in 1220 and became the Althing's lawspeaker for another term in 1222, which he held until the next year. It seems that his fame as an international poet was instrumental in his election. Snorri was by this time an international Nordic celebrity.

Snorri's later political career was aimed at getting Icelanders to rally around his idea of having Iceland vote to accept royal Norwegian control. The comparatively freedom-loving Icelanders were vastly opposed to this (though whether it was on ideological and cultural grounds, or entirely political ones, remains debated). Snorri attempted to marry into another family, to hopefully consolidate his power and influence. Yet as his power grew, so did resistance to it. Snorri seemed to come to the conclusion that the only way to accomplish his goals was through strength and power, and so he gathered an army to achieve his political goals.

It did not go well. Snorri's own brothers were opposed to his actions, and the civil war dragged on. King Haakon IV attempted to intervene by inviting all parties to a peace conference in Norway. Both distance and the state of geography, as well as the stubbornness of the parties involved, who distrusted each other and the king, made this a drawn-out affair. But eventually they met in Norway. Snorri's arrival in Norway made it clear to King Haakon that he was no longer a stable or reliable agent for his will across the sea.

King Haakon IV refused to let Snorri return

to Iceland, afraid that he might cause trouble should he release him. Snorri begged the king, declaring to him, in a phrase imprinted on the Icelandic cultural memory, "út vil ek,": literally "out want I," but meaning "I want to go home." He was allowed to leave, and returned to Iceland in 1239. By then King Haakon IV had his own challenges. Civil war in Iceland no longer concerned him when pretenders to his own throne were gathering forces at home.

The last years of Snorri's life were no less troublesome than the years preceding them. Snorri attempted to restart his political career, but failed. He tried to gather armed supporters, but also failed. It's possible at this point that King Haakon saw Snorri's support of the Icelandic-Norwegian union as being a liability rather than an asset. A plot was afoot to end the liability.

Ironically, Snorri was warned of the plot in runes, but he could not seem to understand them. In autumn of 1241, a man claiming to be an agent of the King of Norway entered Snorri's house and assassinated him.

The death of the celebrity poet was not popular on either side of the Norwegian Sea, and King Haakon IV tried to play it off by saying that he was just trying to arrest Snorri, but things got out of hand. Had Snorri only complied, Haakon insisted, Snorri might have lived. Either way, Haakon continued his campaign of charming Icelandic clan chiefs and Althing members. In 1262, the Althing voted for union with Norway, with each member swearing an oath of personal loyalty to the Norwegian king, a practice which continued until 1662.

But why we care about Snorri Sturluson has little to do with the political history of Iceland or Norway, and everything to do with his poetry. Snorri Sturluson's major concern in life was that the linguistic culture and Norse literary heritage was dying. Like most folklore, the great tales of Norse mythology were primarily oral, locked in the songs and tales, passed across tables, around fires, and through cups. There was also a strong tradition of riddles and kenning that Snorri felt was dying and should be preserved.

To take some small examples: a kenning is an idiomatic phrase to replace a common noun, often for literary or artistic purposes. For example: a kenning for "ocean" might be whale-road, While one for a "lord" would be ring-giver, as Norse lords passed rings to their vassals to seal their relationship. These might seem like small linguistic losses. But, scaling up, Snorri also recorded Viking riddles. For example:

> Who are those twain
> that on ten feet run,
> three their eyes are
> but only one tail?
> This riddle ponder
> O prince Heidrek!

In this riddle one needs to consider what or who has ten legs and three eyes between them. Without knowing anything about Norse mythology, the answer would be near impossible to know. Recall that Odin only had one eye, after plucking one out and setting it into the Well of Mimir. He also had two legs, so we could subtract one eye and two legs from our creature. That still leaves us to find a creature he rode with two eyes and eight legs. The answer was Odin's steed, Sleipnir, a horse with eight legs.

So, the answer to the riddle: Odin riding Sleipnir.

Few of the Norse riddles required as specific answers as this, yet still they are all rooted in the way that Norse language was able to see and understand the world. And Snorri, who was Christian himself, saw this cultural legacy slipping away. He is largely thought to be the single hand most responsible for setting down the Eddas, one poetic and one prose, recording

Norse mythology, serving as the primary source for almost all we know about the Norse mythological canon today. He was also responsible for writing the Heimskringla, the History of the Norwegian Kings.

Snorri was far from the only Icelandic writer. The Norse were one of the most unusually literate pre-modern societies, probably owing at least in part to the significance of their runic alphabet for religion, spirituality, and more generally egalitarian views of their people; also, as a refuge against the monarchies and autocrats of continental Europe, Iceland served as a refuge for those who sought to live outside of royal control, and as a result had a greater freedom to write as they liked.

As a Christian, Snorri's original texts do not outright refer to the Norse gods as literal deities, though it is clear what was intended, and what he understood them to be: an intangible symbol of his people's cultural heritage that was worth protecting and defending.

Three Kingdoms and Kalmar

The flame of paganism died a slow death in Scandinavia. As William and Harald made their bids for the throne of England, Erik the Heathen made the last bid for pagan rule over Scandinavia. As Snorri wrote in the

Heimskringla (Sturluson, n.d. Baptizing the People of Smaland):

At that time there were many people all around in the Swedish dominions who were heathens, and many were bad Christians; for there were some of the kings who renounced Christianity, and continued heathen sacrifices, as Blotsvein [Erik's father], and afterwards Erik [the Heathen], had done.

The practices associated with Norse paganism depleted with a sort of half-life as the Kings of Norway, Denmark, and Sweden converted to Christianity. The conversion of Scandinavia is often described as a "top-down" approach, with the kings of northern Europe enforcing Christian rule on their subjects, though it was a process that took centuries, and oft involved the Norse gods themselves.

St. Anskar, a French Catholic born during the reign of Charlemagne, became Archbishop of Bremen-Hamburg and took it upon himself to journey to take his mission to Scandinavia to try to convert the pagan Norse to Christianity. He was met not with hate or violence, but with diplomacy: He was treated as an honored guest. And his mission, though it would take centuries to complete, earned him the epithet Apostle of the North. Anskar's life is recorded in the aptly named Life of Anskar, by his student Bishop Rimbert. And Rimbert includes mention of some of the methods by which the pagans were converted to Christianity:

They determined that enquiry should be made by the casting of lots in order to discover what was the will of the gods. They went out, therefore, to the plain, in accordance with their custom, and the lot decided that it was the will of God that the Christian religion should be established there. (Chapter XXVII).

In some cases, it seemed that even the pagan gods agreed that Scandinavia should become Christian.

The nobles of Scandinavia sought to counteract the influence of the Hansa, known in English as "The Hanseatic League." The Hansa were a group of powerful merchants who controlled trade from as far as London, down the Rhine, and through the Baltic Sea and into Russia (Hawes, 2018. The Hansa). The Hansa were exceptionally powerful merchant princes, and drove not just trade, but politics and power in the region of northern and central Europe. (For comparison, they would continue to exist in the late 18th Century, and were notable enough even that late that US President John Adams sought to send an ambassador to the Hansa, as if they were a foreign country.)

Scandinavian nobility and royalty decided that they could best counteract the Hansa together, and beginning in 1397, through a series of marriages, laws, and personal commitments united the thrones of Norway, Denmark, and Sweden (Lunde, 2014. Introduction). In effect, since Finland was mostly under the rule of the Swedish crown, Iceland affirmed their loyalty to the Norwegian monarchy, and what remained of the Greenlandic colonies paid homage to Norway. This effectively united the entire Nordic world into a single political unit.

However, the Kingdoms of Norway, Sweden, and Denmark were not dissolved into this new "Kalmar Union." They were merely united into the role of a single monarch and acted as one (ibid.).

This Union was inherently unstable, but surprisingly durable. The nobility of Scandinavia, wanting to keep the German-dominated Hansa at bay, found that giving more power to the monarchy was a bit of a deal with the devil. The monarchy, of course, was happy to oblige, having their power expand from the Russian steppe all the way into the Norwegian Sea and into continental Europe. Denmark at the time controlled the province of Holstein, today in northern Germany.

The Kalmar Union was rocky and problematic essentially from the get-go. The division was drawn across national lines, particularly between the Danes and the Swedes. Violence, coups, and outright civil war were common between the supposedly united kingdoms all throughout the 1400s. In 1520, as Sweden threatened to leave the Union, the Danish King Christian II invaded with an army, defeated the Swedish separatists, and had himself crowned King of Sweden to keep the Union in his person (Lunde, 2014. Chapter 1). He followed up his coronation by executing the rivals who didn't support his power and reign in what is known as the Stockholm Bloodbath (Lunde, 2014. Introduction).

Gustav of the House of Vasa, whose father was killed in the Bloodbath, assembled an army and renewed the war. He led the Swedish War of Liberation, which achieved victory in 1523, when Gustav was crowned King Gustav I of Sweden (ibid.). Separated, this is the end of the Kalmar Union, but not the end of the dream of Nordic Unity. Danish Kings tried to restore the Kalmar Union through conquest, but were unable to do so. They were able to solidify their rule over Norway by uniting Denmark-Norway into a union not dissimilar to the way Scotland and England were united in the 1800s (until Norway was later transferred back to Swedish rule for the remainder of the 19th Century). Kalmar, a mostly-failed experiment, did not lead to a lasting Nordic Empire, but it did lead to the meteoric rise of the Vasa Dynasty and the Swedish Empire.

CHAPTER 4
THE RISE AND FALL OF THE SWEDISH EMPIRE

At the end of the 10th Century, a skald by the name of Steinunn Refsdottir in Iceland taunted a Nordic Christian missionary by the name of Thangbrandr (Dasent, 1861. 98. Of Thangbrand and Gudleif). In her verses, she mentioned how the missionary's ship, wrecked in a storm, was the result of Thor, and that Christ didn't offer any help to the missionary's efforts.

She even tried to turn the tables on Thangbrandr, telling him he'd be better off as a pagan: "Did you ever hear," she asked, "how Thor challenged Christ to a duel, and Christ did not dare accept the challenge?"

If Thor did indeed challenge Christ to a duel, we don't know the results. We know that the Norse long thought that Christ was a "dead" god.

After all, that was the impression they got, having seen his image hanging from crosses in monasteries, churches, and abbeys across Europe. And we know that the Norse were perfectly comfortable living alongside Christians. One well-preserved artifact from a smithy in Denmark shows a mold with one side depicting a cross (for those who wanted an icon for Christ), and the other a hammer (for those who wanted an icon for Thor) (Smith, 2018. p. 5). Clearly, to the smith, money was money whether it came from a Christian or a heathen.

We do not know who came out on top between Thor and Jesus, but we do know that Christ very much won the battle on Earth. From Ireland to Russia and all the way to the New World, the Vikings and their descendants converted to Christianity and settled into a world that would have been unfamiliar to their forebears.

In an odd way, Ragnarok had come. The strange winter broke, battles from Stamford Bridge and Hastings to Paris to Constantinople to the last stand of paganism from Erik the Heathen were held, and the gods joined their fallen Vikings in oblivion.

At the end of Ragnarok, after all of the Aesir, Vanir, jotuns, and all their warriors were dead, the world as we knew it effectively ended. But all was not lost in the myth: A single woman and a single man, Lif and Lifthrasir respectively, emerged from a tree, called after the fires of Surtr abated, and set about to repopulate the earth (Larrington, 2014. p. 47).

It is likely pure coincidence that Snorri Sturluson recorded the end of the Norse world as a man, a woman, and a tree with the mission to be fruitful and multiply, and that this is also how the Biblical Book of Genesis begins. But even so, life imitates art. The Viking world ended, and in its place was a Christianized one that the Norse had adapted to, just as Christendom had once adapted to the Norse.

And it had come with its own fire and violence.

The House of Vasa and the Reformation

When Gustav I freed Sweden from Danish rule (or unjustly conquered Sweden from its rightful Danish King, if you prefer), he established the House of Vasa (Lunde, 2014. Introduction). Gustav led the war against the Danish Kings and freed Sweden from Danish rule, though it is key to note that there were both theocratic and democratic elements to his rise as King of Sweden. Gustav did not singularly seize the crown and declare himself king, but handed power over "his" "new" realm to a privy council. The council was set to elect a new King, though it was to be an uncontested election: Gustav was the only real candidate. And even then, visiting German supporters declared Gustav's election as King of Sweden to be the "will of God" (Peterson, 2014. p. 31). On the 6th of June, 1523, the votes were counted and Gustav was declared King of Sweden. Though he was still not crowned (the traditional marker of the transfer of a Price-Elect's/Heir Apparent's rise), this is the date traditionally seen as the beginning of King Gustav I's reign, celebrated since 1983 as the National Day of Sweden.

While the Kalmar Union was breaking apart, another, much larger storm was beginning on continental Europe. For generations the Catholic Church ran on a system of "indulgences," where the wealthy could effectively buy their way into heaven by literally paying for their sins. If one sinned, they could simply pay an amount of money to the church, and receive a letter saying they had been absolved of their sins. This system had become so corrupted that it was almost impossible to notice (see Macculloch, 2010. Chapter 17 - A House Divided).

Enter the German monk Martin Luther. Luther saw this corrupt system for what it was, and tried to work through channels in the church to reform it. However, he was rebuffed at every turn. In 1517, he nailed a copy of his famous treatise, referred to as The Ninety-Five Theses, to the door of the cathedral at Worms. In 1521, he was excommunicated for his blistering criticism of the Catholic Church, and this marked the beginning of the Protestant Reformation (Man, 2010).

Prior to Luther, there were many attempts at splintering reformed movements in the Catholic world. The Lollards, referenced multiple times in Chaucer's The Canterbury Tales, disapproved of Catholic hegemony and promoted a sort of folk-Catholicism where local traditions and ideas took precedence over Church authority (Macculloch, 2010. Chapter 16 - Perspectives on the True Church). The Hussites, called such because they followed the teachings of the Bohemian reformer Jan Hus, were the immediate predecessors to the Protestant Reformation. Hus's teachings spread across central Europe until the Church responded with extreme violence in what are now known as the Hussite Wars, lasting from 1419 to 1434 (ibid.). The Hussite Wars, other than leading to the devastation of Hungary and the rise of the

House of Hapsburg, also taught the victorious Catholic Church a lesson: When heretics become too big to hunt down, the only way to end the heresy is through war.

One of the big reasons for the breakup of the Kalmar Union was the perceived influence that Holstein Germans had, to the expense of Swedish interests (Peterson, 2014. p. 31). Ironically, German supporters immediately began to influence ideas that would be fundamental to both the rule of the House of Vasa and the future of Scandinavia as a whole. Luther's ideas spread like wildfire, especially after his excommunication by Roman authorities, and a few of those supporters of Luther's ideas made their way to Sweden and Gustav's council (Lunde, 2014. Introduction).

In 1526, the first Swedish translation of the New Testament was published (The Editors of Encyclopaedia Britannica, 1998). Later that same year, King Gustav tried to broker a council between his court priest and a representative from Rome. The latter refused, saying that Church matters were not up for royal discussion. This led to the Riksdag of Vasteras in 1527, known as the "Reformation Riksdag."

This was not the end of the Reformation in Sweden but the beginning. King Gustav I continued to act independently of the will of the Roman Church, further acting against their will with the message: Submit to the will of the crown, or leave. For the next century, the church would find it harder and harder to maintain influence in Sweden in any meaningful capacity, eventually turning it into a Protestant nation.

Over the next century of Vasa rule, their House would not stay isolated in Scandinavia, either. It began when Gustav's son John married Catherine of House Jagiellon, a Polish princess. Catherine had a son, Sigismund. And by his mother's line, Sigismund ascended to the throne of the Polish-Lithuanian Commonwealth in 1587 (Lunde, 2014. Introduction). Meanwhile his father, John, deposed his uncle, Eric (both sons of Gustav I). But both John and Eric continued their father's seizure of power from the Roman Church in support of a developing Protestant Sweden. Sigismund, now King Sigismund III, was a devout Catholic (ibid.). And seeing as he was directly in line for the throne of Sweden, this spelled trouble.

In 1592, Sigismund inherited the throne of Sweden from his father, John III, and became King Sigismund I of Sweden. Sigismund intended on invading his paternal homeland and reestablishing Church control through a counter-reformation (Peterson, 2014. Chapter 10). His invasion was met with intense resistance in the uncreatively titled "War Against Sigismund." Sigismund's Polish forces were defeated in 1598, and he fled Sweden, out of fear for his life, shortly after the armistice was signed. In 1599, the Riksdag assembled and officially deposed Sigismund, electing in his place Gustav I's third son, the Duke Charles, who became King Charles IX (Lunde, 2014. Introduction).

The consolidation of Charles's reign did not end the religious bloodshed in Sweden. He had the remainder of Sigismund's supporters gathered and executed, and the last vestiges of Roman control in Sweden were officially severed. Sweden had become a completely Lutheran country, with remaining church holdings turned over to the Church of Sweden (ibid.). But the memory of the Polish invasion and the animosity towards Catholicism would persist for some time.

The House of Vasa in Poland continued to expand and become intertwined with the nobility and politics of eastern Europe, including in Russia, though this branch of the family had only retained a vague memory of their origins in Sweden, and remained thoroughly non-Nordic in terms of religion, culture, language, and politics. (Though it is somewhat ironic that Slavicized Swedish royalty returned to power in Russia, albeit briefly.)

Meanwhile in north-central Europe, things had reached a boiling point. Charles IX passed the throne of Sweden to his son Gustav Adolf in 1611, who was crowned King Gustav II. He would become known by his latinized name and epithet Gustavus Adolphus the Great.

When King Gustav II came to his throne, the Kingdom of Sweden stretched into most of modern Finland, and the northern coast of Estonia, though the southern tip of Sweden, the island of Gotland, and the mountains of central Sweden were still controlled by Denmark-Norway (Lunde, 2014. Chapter 1). By the time Gustav II's reign ended, the Swedish Empire had expanded into what is today St. Petersburg in Russia, and had seized ports on the Baltic and North Sea coasts of Germany and Poland as Sweden was drawn into the most destructive conflict in Europe before the World Wars: the Thirty Years' War.

In 1618, princes of the vast and diverse Holy Roman Empire were starting to convert to Protestantism, while others remained loyal to the Catholic Church and persecuted Protestants in their realm. Protestant princes turned the tables and sponsored counter-persecutions. Things came to a head in 1618 when two Catholics were thrown from a Prague tower window during negotiations with local Protestant leaders. The two miraculously survived. Catholics said that angels lowered them safely to the ground below. Protestants wrote that they fell into a dung heap. Whichever story one believed, both Catholics and Protestants knew that it was a sign of a division that could not be healed (Macculloch, 2010. Chapter 17 - A House Divided).

The Thirty Years' War began as a relatively simple religious conflict: Protestant vs. Catholic. But as the powers of Europe from Spain, France, England, Poland, and Sweden were drawn into it, it became much more a struggle for power as Catholics and Protestants allied with each other to get a handle over their coreligionist competitors for power (Hawes, 2018. Part Four: Apocalypse). The War was so devastating and destructive that those who witnessed it thought the end times of the Book of Revelation had arrived.

Sweden escaped relatively unscathed. However, as the battlefront in the defense of Protestant faith, King Gustav II used it as the staging ground for the expansion of Swedish military might, and the flexing of Swedish power.

Gustav II is often known as "the Father of Modern Warfare," as he experimented with a standing army that was held to a high moral standard (Lunde, 2014. Chapter 7). This was in opposition to standard European practices at the time, which fought their wars mainly through mercenary powers who often achieved their payment through the sacking of cities and the despoiling of entire countrysides. He also pioneered systematic and creative combinations of infantry, cavalry, and firearms, which became increasingly central to the way warfare was fought (Lunde, 2014. Chapter 2).

A full analysis of the Thirty Years' War is far beyond the scope of this text. However, one of its casualties was King Gustav II, who died in 1632 at the Battle of Lützen, though the War in Germany would rage until 1648, when it was concluded in the Peace of Westphalia, changing the way international diplomacy was done forever by developing the concept of Westphalian Statehood (Lunde, 2014. Chapter 7). Gustav II, after all he had done in defense of his faith, is recognized by Protestants across European history as one of their great defenders

(Trueman, 2015). It is possible that without him, Protestantism might not have been wiped out of history, but it might have struggled more in Germany, and a different outcome to the war might have resulted.

King Gustav II left the throne to his daughter, Christina. She was only six when her father was shot multiple times at Luetzen. A regency council ruled over her until she reached her majority in 1644, at which point she reigned as Crown Princess, and then as Queen in 1650 when she was crowned Queen of Sweden. Queen Christina was an erudite woman, fond of reading books about mathematics, philosophy, alchemy, and religion (Lunde, 2014. Chapter 6). She was known as "the Minerva of the North" for her learning, and in her reign, having invited so many scholars and funded new universities, Stockholm became "the Athens of the North."

It was also through her own erudition that Queen Christina brought about the end of her own reign. She became convinced of the truth of Catholicism and secretly converted in Brussels. Shortly thereafter she publicly announced her conversion in a visit to Innsbruck. Unlike her cousin Sigismund, Queen Christina decided not to attempt to re-force Catholicism on her country. She chose to abdicate in favor of her cousin, Charles. In an elaborate ceremony, Queen Christina wore all of her regal finery, which was stripped of her and put on Charles. The last item on her was her crown, which she removed herself and relinquished. Charles was dressed and crowned as King Charles X later that day (ibid.).

Ex-queen Christina left Sweden in the following days and settled in Rome. The Pope referred to her as "the queen without a country" and when she died, she was interred in St. Peter's Basilica (Stephan, 2019).

The Protestant Reformation was long over in Sweden, and she would not be returning to the Catholic orbit. In less than a century after it had happened, Sweden had risen to become a verified, centralized empire serving as its new faith's primary defender, and Nordic power had even stretched across the Atlantic. Again.

New Sweden: Return to Vinland

By the middle of the 1600s, the Spanish and Portuguese Empires had completed their initial overseas expansion, and more northern European powers had started to get into the colonial game. France laid claim to islands in the Caribbean, and the Mississippi and St. Lawrence River Valleys. The Dutch likewise claimed their fair share of the Caribbean and traded a small sum for the island of Manhattan, which they claimed as New Amsterdam. The English began experimenting with capitalism, subsidizing companies trying to set up colonies in Massachusetts and Virginia before expanding across the rest of North America. Sweden, now achieving new heights of hard and soft power, decided to try their own hand at developing an American colony.

In 1626, in the reign of Gustav II, the Swedish South Company was founded with the goal to establish Swedish colonies between Florida and Newfoundland (Jameson & Johnson, 1912). Between 1638 and 1655, a total of 11 expeditions were sent to the New World in an effort of establishing a colony, to the most mild of successes (Covart, 2016).

The first expedition left Gothenburg in 1637 and sailed to the Gulf of Delaware. The swath of land around the Delaware River that the expedition claimed ran into the territory claimed by the Dutch (ibid.). However, the (colonial) populations of both New Sweden and New Amsterdam were so small, and the territory remained largely unsurveyed.

This was not to last. In later expeditions, the colony became lightly peopled by Europeans. Some 600 Europeans came to populate the colony. A member of the Dutch Minuit family became the colony's first governor (the Minuits were also heavily involved in the establishment and governance of New Amsterdam). The Swedish authorities didn't seek to firm up their boundary with the Dutch colony, knowing full well that their claimed borders overlapped, but the Dutch sought to concentrate their population on Manhattan.

In its short existence, the colony never stopped developing. Governor Minuit summoned sachems (chiefs) of the Delaware and Susquehannock tribes to firm up their own political relationship. The boundary they drew for the colony extended towards the Schuylkill River (in modern Philadelphia) and over coastal Maryland (giving the Swedish colony a border dispute with the budding English colony there). Forts were built across the colony, and the Swedes even supported their new indigenous allies in their war against Maryland colony (Jennings, 1984. p. 120). For a brief time, it seemed like the ascension of Sweden in Europe would be recreated in the New World.

Trying to take advantage of events in Europe, the Dutch sent an armed squadron of ships and men to seize the Swedish colony (Brown, 2018). In the summer of 1655, the

Dutch army marched into the Delaware River Valley and captured Fort Trinity and Fort Christina. New Sweden became officially incorporated into New Amsterdam in 1655 (Blom, 2014). The Swedish and Finnish settlers of the colony, however, retained local autonomy, maintaining their own militia, court, lands, and following their own religious rites (though the Dutch were Protestant themselves, regardless).

This ended in 1669 when the entirety of the colony of New Netherlands, including their captured New Sweden, was conquered by the English (Blom, 2014). Most of what was once New Sweden was, however, still Swedish and Finnish. This led Marcus Jacobsson to attempt to start an armed rebellion to return New Sweden to the rightful rule of the Kingdom of Sweden. For his height, he was known as "the Long Swede," and his rebellion "the Revolt of the Long Swede." His revolution failed and Marcus was sold into slavery in the Caribbean (Haefeli, 2006).

New Sweden continued to exist in an unofficial manner. A Swedish log cabin, located on Society Hill, was built in what is now Philadelphia in 1669. It was used as a church until about 1700, when a proper church, Gloria

Dei, was built on the site (National Historic Site Pennsylvania, 2021). The church, in honor of its history, unofficially calls it "Old Swedes' Church." By 1682, Delaware, New Jersey, and lastly Pennsylvania had all received royal charters from the English Crown. New Sweden was never formally dissolved, but it was effectively partitioned between the three future American States (Sprinchorn, 1884).

The big wave of Nordic emigration to North America wouldn't begin until the late 19th Century, but New Sweden stirred the Nordic imagination and generated interest in the New World. The political, cultural, and demographic influence of the Swedes in the early colonial period in America is incomparable to the Spanish, French, English, or even Dutch, but there are still many places that retain the historic legacy of Swedish influence in the area. Swedesboro, NJ; Swedesburg, PA; Christiana, DE; Upland, PA; and Swedeland, PA remain some of the most prominent examples.

Another contribution the Swedes brought to America was the log cabin. The log cabin was an architectural design so emblematic of the American frontier, culminating in the early life and legacy of President Abraham Lincoln, born in a Kentucky log cabin in 1809, that it is thought to be authentically American. However, the oldest surviving log cabin on American soil is located on the appropriately named Swedesboro-Paulsboro Rd. in Gibbstown, NJ. It was, in fact, a design brought over by Nordic colonists (Solomon, 2021).

The Deluge

Charles X came to the throne of Sweden after his cousin Christina abdicated the throne, by virtue of his uncle Gustav II. As the son of Gustav's sister, Catherine, Charles X signaled a change of dynasty in Sweden, as a member of the (German) House of Wittelsbach. He reigned from his cousin's abdication in 1654 to 1660. During his short reign, he was in charge of possibly the single most destructive period of Nordic history. The Viking Age included.

The Polish-Lithuanian Commonwealth was born centuries earlier when the female King Jadwiga (no, not a Queen; she was crowned Jadwiga Rex, as Polish law didn't allow a Queen to assume the throne) married the Lithuanian monarch upon his conversion to Catholicism (Zamoyski, 2009. TWO Between East and West). Their new country was large and dominative, and like the Swedes over the last century, the Polish Jagiellon Dynasty had expanded into Hungary, Germany, and Russia before that role was taken over by the House of Vasa (Zamoyski, 2009. THREE The Jagiellon Experience).

Moreso than even the Swedish nobility "confirming" their Kings in an electoral process, the Polish-Lithuanian monarchs were chosen in an aristocratic election by the Polish legislature. There were few restrictions on who the sejm could vote for, and as a result the Polish-Lithuanian democratic experiment descended into corruption that would end with disastrous consequences multiple times (Zamoyski, 2009. FOUR Religion and Politics). This inherent weakness would first be exploited by the Swedes.

Almost immediately upon being crowned, Charles X made plans for the invasion of Poland (Zamoyski, 2009. NINE A Biblical Flood). He sailed across the Baltic with his armies and landed on the northern coast of Poland, marching quickly to Warsaw to seize the capital and then set out to occupy the majority of central Poland. King John II Casimir (of the House of Vasa) fled Poland to German Silesia. Polish nobility defected to the Swedish army, including many of the famous Winged Hussars (Bain, 1911).

The Swedish army and its defectors marched

farther south towards Krakow. There the war started to turn against Charles. Though he continued to win battle after battle, attrition and guerilla warfare began to stress and weaken his forces. Charles came to the conclusion that he might defeat the Poles in the field, but he could not conquer Poland this way.

Whether it was by design or just a result of their attempt at conquest remains to be proved. But what resulted was the greatest destruction in Poland until World War II (and, by some estimates, including World War II). Some demographers have estimated that between one-third and half of the Polish population was killed in the violence that followed (Zamoyski, 2009. NINE A Biblical Flood). Surely, the Swedish Protestants did not forget the attempted forcible conquest and conversion of their homeland by the ancestor of the very king they were fighting against. The destruction of Poland was so thorough that the conflict is most well-known not by the more historical name "The Second Northern War," but as the Deluge, describing how the country was so completely covered and buried under violence and destruction (Sienkiewicz, 2017. The Deluge: Introduction).

One of the most lasting effects of the Deluge

was the rapine of cultural artifacts from Poland to Scandinavia. Polish records, valuables from palaces and estates, artwork, the entire Royal Library, and libraries from all across the country were despoiled and their contents taken back to Scandinavia (Zamoyski, 2009. NINE A Biblical Flood). The original works by Nicholas Copernicus, the original designer of a heliocentric model for the solar system, were taken from their homeland (Naylor, 2017). For over three centuries, these items were never returned. The vast majority of them remain in universities and museums in different parts of Uppsala. Their return to their homeland is unlikely.

It is notable that while the Swedish area of conquest in the Deluge was more populated, and has been considered the worst affected, they did not act alone. Russia invaded the eastern half of the country and behaved much the same way (though to less effect, as Sweden's conquests held the major population and economic centers). Poland, suffering at the hands of the Protestants, ended its long period of religious liberty and pluralism, and ejected Protestants from their territory upon the war's conclusion (Zamoyski, 2009. NINE A Biblical Flood). The intense weakening of the country was not even to the great long-term benefit of

Sweden, but of Russia. The Tsarist state, with its greatest western rival brought low, was set on an upward trajectory.

A trajectory that put it in the path of the Swedish Empire.

The Great Northern War

At the turn of the 18th Century, Sweden was very much one of the greatest powers in Europe, in league with the rising powers of England and France, and the historic power of Spain. The Swedish Empire, thanks to Gustav II in particular, had a virtually unstoppable army and an empire that turned the Baltic into a lake all their own (Extra Credits, 2017a). Charles X left his short reign to his son, crowned Charles XI, who reigned for nearly four decades. In 1697, he died and left the throne to his fourteen year-old son, crowned Charles XII (Lunde, 2014. Chapter 7).

Empires are not created without creating enemies, and the rise of the Swedish Empire, from a rebel kingdom out from under the Danish thumb, to their wars overseas, against the Dutch, Russians, and Polish, had earned them quite a few. Tsar Peter I, known as "the Great," was the Russian Tsar who turned his empire westwards, breaking the dominating influence of his country's traditional, conservative nobility, forcing everyone to wear pants, and then turning his country, literally, westwards (Galeotti, 2021. 4: Money is the Artery of War). Peter sought to expand Russia into western(ish) Europe, seizing land on the Baltic to open Russian ports to seagoing trade, and to treat with western European powers as equals. So while Charles XII was undergoing his coronation, his education, and puberty, Peter the Great secretly negotiated with the Polish and the Danes to take Sweden down a peg.

In 1700, without Peter's approval, the Danish and Polish forces launched an attack that crossed the Swedish borders. Their attack was ill-organized and poorly commanded (Extra Credits, 2017b). When the Swedes counterattacked, the Polish army shattered and their general was killed (Lunde, 2014. Chapter 8). When the Danes launched an amphibious surprise attack, young Charles himself led the defense and decimated the Danish navy. The Danes were in full retreat and made a separate peace with the Swedes (ibid.).

Peter knew that while the Swedes were busy and probably feeling a bit high on victory, it would be the perfect time to launch his own invasion of Swedish territory before they could regroup. However, he was busy trying to wrap up a war with the Ottoman Turks to his south, and the proud Ottomans were not eager to make peace (Lunde, 2014. Chapter 9). When peace finally did come in the south, Peter wasted no time and gathered his forces to descend upon the Swedish Empire's most eastern provinces. But the delay had forced him to attack in the wet autumn and the frigid winter, and the Swedes had had months to prepare.

Still, even with all of their preparation, the Swedish forces were vastly outnumbered. Charles, however, wasn't deterred. He ordered his forces out into a blizzard to attack the Russians when they least expected it. Swedish victory at the Battle of Narva, at the time deemed impossible, was a devastating blow to the Russians (Lunde, 2014. Chapter 4). The Tsar's army retreated, and Peter was certain that Charles would advance into Russia, possibly to unseat the Tsar himself in Moscow. But Charles instead turned his forces to Poland as he had determined that the Polish had not yet suffered enough by Swedish hands (Lunde, 2014. Chapter 8).

Every battle, betrayal, and campaign of the Great Northern War would be too much to recount here. The war lasted from 1700 to 1721, and in addition to the original combatants of

Sweden, Poland-Lithuania, Russia, and Denmark-Norway, the fighting drew in the Ottoman Empire, the Dutch Republic, Great Britain, and half of Germany, while both sides also allied and funded rebels in the others' territory as far as Ukraine and the Caucasus (Zamoyski, 2009. ELEVEN The Reign of Anarchy).

The war claimed the lives of about a half-million people, including the young and bull-headed Charles XII (Lunde, 2014. Chapter 9). Though he had spent most of his life as a wartime monarch, Charles never failed to lead from the frontlines. He was inspecting the trenches of a fortress near the Norwegian border when he was sniped at and shot in the head. The King of Sweden was killed instantly in 1718. Charles XII never married and left no legitimate children (or even illegitimate children, as far as any historian has managed to identify) and so he was succeeded by his sister Ulrika Eleonora. Queen Ulrika found the stress of the throne unsuitable to her constitution, and she abdicated in favor of her German husband Frederick of the House Hesse-Kassel. At this time, the Riksdag had mostly stripped the monarchy (which they were used to watching getting lost in the Balkans, or on campaign in Ukraine, or laying siege to Polish cities) of its powers and were deep in peace negotiations (Lunde, 2014. Summary and Conclusions).

Multiple treaties were signed to end the war. Sweden's east Baltic possessions (Livonia, Estonia, and parts of Russia) were ceded to the Tsar's control. Prussia (modern east Germany) took possession of Sweden's ports and territories on the southern Baltic. And just as the sun began to set on the Swedish Empire, the end of the war saw the open declaration of the Russian Empire (Galeotti, 2021. 4: Money is the Artery of War). It was an ascendance that would last nearly four centuries.

The End of the Swedish Empire

The Great Northern War, ending with the death of one of Sweden's greatest monarchs, the stripping of monarchical power, the humiliation of Swedish territories by their adversaries, and the rise of a new Empire on their shore, is usually regarded as the end of the Swedish Empire (Morgan, 2021). But there was one more blow yet to be had.

Two wars in the 18th Century saw the occupation of what is today Finland by Russian forces. For centuries Swedish settlers, merchants, and administrators had surveyed Finnish lands and held the territory as the eastern appendage to the Swedish Empire. In what is known as the "Great Wrath" in Finland, i.e. the Finnish theater of the Great Northern War, Russian forces occupied Finland, only to return it in the Treaty of Stockholm in 1721 (Kujala, 2000). The "Lesser Wrath" came some two decades later, with a relatively short war instigated by the same political party (called "the Hats") that signed the peace treaties with Russia a generation earlier (The Age of Enlightenment - Finland, n.d.). The war was relatively short, and was partially a side-show in the wider War of Austrian Succession, but ended in disaster for Sweden, with another occupation of Finland and cession of more territory, but also with the withdrawal of Russian forces from Finland (Scott, 2011).

A third war between Russia and Sweden (1788–1790) convinced the Finnish people that their future with Sweden was precarious. The memory of the Great Wrath had so thoroughly decimated a generation of Finnish men during the Russian burning of Helsinki and the wanton destruction of the countryside that it was not believed their country had recovered, almost a century later (The Editors of Encyclopaedia Britannica, 1998a).

Though Finns go back in history for many centuries, this was the beginning of an awakening to Finnish national and cultural identity, though it would take another century for a serious Finnish independence movement to form and reach fruition. Still, the other option of nationality to Finns in the late 18th Century was just as distasteful as their previous centuries. Today regarded mainly as a traitor, who defected to Russia and served the Tsarina Catherine the Great, Count Georg Magnus Sprengtporten conceived the idea for an autonomous Finnish territory in the Russian Empire. Said Sprengtporten, "We are not Swedes, we do not want to become Russians, let us, therefore, be Finns" (Wilson, 1976. Chapter 3).

Enter Napoleon.

Napoleon had gone through a campaign of conquest in Europe for almost two decades by the time he met Tsar Alexander I on a raft in Poland in 1807. The French and Russian Emperors decided (much as Europe would be divided again a century-and-a-half later at Yalta) that Europe would be divided into a western zone of influence where France would dominate, and an eastern zone where Russia would. Napoleon's main requirement for agreeing to leave the east out of his empire was that Russia must abide by the "Continental

System." The Continental System was Napoleon's weapon to isolate and hopefully starve his main rival, Britain. The Continental System entirely forbade British goods and merchants from being bought or sold on the European continent (Zamoyski, 2018. 30. Master of Europe). Barring an outright invasion of England, it was Napoleon's best weapon to try to end British influence in Europe.

The ultra-religious King of Sweden, Gustav IV of House Holstein-Gottorp, saw Napoleon as the antichrist, and was unwilling to abandon his ally and main trading partner, Britain (Frilund, n.d.). Which is why, when he received the Tsar's letter demanding that Sweden abide by the Continental System if they were to continue peaceful relations across the Baltic Sea, it made war practically inevitable.

Compared to the previous wars between Russia and Sweden, this one was comparatively short—just over a year-and-a-half long—and the combatants were few. Sweden launched an attack against Denmark, supported by Britain, while Russia counterattacked, supported from afar by France. When it was over, the results were decisive: Russia was in full control of Finland. The Treaty of Fredrikshamn made it official: Sweden lost a full third of its territory, which became inaugurated in the Russian Empire as the Grand Duchy of Finland (Zamoyski, 2018. 35. Apogee).

The Russian and Western stars would continue to rise, culminating in the World Wars, in which Scandinavian countries would play extremely minor roles. The sun had very much set on the political years of Scandinavian power. Sweden's century as the Giant of the North and continued influence as a Great Power until the Napoleonic era was certainly a recasting of their previous role and power as Viking raiders, setting out to transform the world from one era to another. For the 19th and 20th Centuries, Scandinavia played a much quieter role in world history.

CHAPTER 5
SCANDINAVIA IN THE MODERN WORLD

After Napoleon's final defeat at Waterloo in 1815, Sweden, which had been anti-Napoleon, managed to get a seat at the Congress of Vienna. The Congress stripped Norway from their pro-Napoleon rival, Denmark, and handed it to Stockholm's control.

Finland, however, remained under Russian dominion. Relations between Napoleon and the Tsar had deteriorated, resulting in Napoleon's disastrous invasion of Russia, in which a brutal war of primarily scorched-earth tactics annihilated Napoleon's army, with tens of thousands freezing to death in the Russian winter (Zamoyski, 2012). Russia would oppose Napoleon all the way to Waterloo. Ironically, this ultimately put Russia and Sweden on the same side of the table in Vienna.

Iceland, long under Norwegian dominion, was transferred to Denmark ahead of time, and so, after Vienna, the Icelandic Althing paid loyalty and homage to the Danish monarch in Copenhagen (Arnórsdóttir, 2019). It was also around this time that the Danish, upset at their loss of Norway but not eager to march back to the battlefield, began expanding northwards. Scandinavian ships and explorers returned to Greenland after nearly four centuries of abandoning the world's largest island (Lambert, 2021). The exploration of the territory would continue until well into the 20th Century, and its territory wouldn't be fully demarcated until 2022 after a long-standing border dispute with Canada (Chase, 2022).

Scandinavia had very much entered the modern age. The politics of power in Europe had moved away from Scandinavian power and interests, but the forces of industrialization and modernization would still spread across the Nordic countries—most of which, at the Congress of Vienna in 1815, were under foreign occupation. The road from pre-modern societies being defeated multiple times at the hands of foreign powers to becoming some of the most free, progressive, and developed economies in the world serves as an inspiration to countries around the globe.

The Danish Empire

The 1800s are often referred to as "the Long 19th Century" because it was an era of intense and rapid change. For example, in 1800 the United States was barely a quarter of its present size, extending from the Atlantic Ocean to an ill-defined western border on the Mississippi River. A journey from one end to the other was exceptionally dangerous. A century later, the United States would expand beyond, all the way to the Pacific coast, and was in possession of territories scattered across the Pacific Ocean—Hawai'i, the Philippines, and Guam—and was conquering and establishing client regimes in the Caribbean and across Latin America.

Europe would undergo similar levels of expansion. First there would be a brief retreat. Portugal and Spain, due at least in part to Napoleon, saw their possessions in the New World declare independence one-by-one until the Empires were shadows of their former selves.

Yet the expansion of European empires was not over. Britain was already in the process of taking over all (or essentially all) of both India and Australia, and their remaining North American possession (Canada) was expanding westwards along with the United States. France, though humbled at Waterloo, was about to have its third act in imperialism, mainly spreading across Africa, Southeast Asia, and the South Pacific.

Closer to Scandinavia, Russia had reached its maximum territorial extent. Their experiment in conquering Finland and establishing a vassal state worked out so well that the Tsars established a "Kingdom of Poland" (and added it to their own collection of crowns).

Sweden's acquisition of Norway at the Congress of Vienna was to be their last major territorial acquisition. And even this was muted. The Swedish-Norwegian merger was not a military conquest, but a United Kingdom of two nations under a single monarch (Elloway, 2013. Nationalism & Identity). Ironically, the Danish dream of the Kalmar Union mocked them from across the sea.

Denmark experienced their own minor expansion as well. European powers took some time to do to Africa what they had already done in the Americas, culminating in the Berlin Conference in 1888, when European powers met in Germany to divide the continent before a misunderstanding in Africa led to war in Europe.

Prior to this literal carving up of the world, however, European powers sent missions to Africa to establish trading posts and minor colonies. Denmark, returning to their historic roots as a sea power, was relatively active in building forts along the West African coastline (Brimnes, 2021). Some of these forts were built as early as the mid-17th century, but as the shipping lanes became more crowded and the world economy became more intertwined, so did the desire for more ports of harbor with one's flag flying from the docks. Denmark built a number of forts mainly in what is today Ghana, but the vast majority that survived into the 19th century were sold to Britain in 1850, incorporated into the colony called the "British Gold Coast" (Carstensen, 2010). Notably, one of the forts that Denmark had built, maintaining its Scandinavian name, Fort Christiansborg, until it received a native name, Osu Castle, houses the offices for the President of Ghana (Visit Ghana, n.d.).

Denmark had also been involved in the New World trade since the 1500s. The Danish West India Company purchased islands from France as far back as the 1600s, giving Danish traders (including slave traders) ports of harbor in the New World. The Danish West Indies soon became reliant on sugar production (Gibson,

2015. Chapter Four). The demographics of the island, so far from Europe and reliant on cheap labor, were always complex. Violent uprisings in the 19th Century, by a largely English-speaking minority, turned the islands into more of a liability and an economic burden on the Danish homeland (Gibson, 2015. Chapter Eight). When the United States made to buy the three islands from Denmark in 1916, the Danish government happily voted in favor of handing the islands over to the United States in exchange for $25 million. The three formerly Danish islands, St. Thomas, St. John, and St. Croix—just west of their sibling Puerto Rico—have been held since 1917 as an organized, unincorporated territory of the United States: the United States Virgin Islands (Grey, 2014).

The Danish maritime empire expanded into Asia, with equally mixed results. Denmark established trading posts in India. The largest of these was the settlement of Tranquebar in modern Tamil Nadu. There was also Balasore in modern Odiya and Serampore in Bengal (Fihl & Lillelund, 2015). Other smaller posts and factories were operated in the 17th and 18th Centuries, but these were the only ones that remained by the mid-19th Century. Even these were enough for Denmark to make a significant profit and investment into their local economies.

As the industrial revolution expanded across Europe, Scandinavia—relatively safe from the political upheavals elsewhere on the continent—was able to devote a large amount of their economies to development (see Jörberg, 1965). And Denmark did it with the profits fueled from their modest trade in India.

It all ended in 1845, when Britain was attempting a first round of consolidation on their Indian Empire. The British more or less forced Denmark to sell the rights to all of their properties on the Indian subcontinent (Carey, 1907. Chapter XIV). Denmark maintained rights over the Nicobar Islands, a small archipelago just off the coast of Burma, but the colonies maintained there struggled to find footing. Denmark sold the rights they had to the colonies to their constant customers, the British, in 1868 (East India Company et al., 1869, p. 191). Even today, the islands (now under the control of the Republic of India) are sparsely populated: some, like North Sentinel Island, only by hostile indigenous groups who never even knew their island crossed any borders (K. N. Smith, 2018).

The final blow to the Danish colonial empire was arguably the independence of Iceland (see below) but the signs of the empire's decline were already there in the middle of the 19th Century, as it was selling colonial possessions to larger powers and was pushed out of the sealanes. In 1848, revolutions swept through much of continental Europe, and hit Germany particularly hard (Hawes, 2018. The Failed Revolution of 1848-9). The social upheaval led to the First Schleswig War, in which northern German principalities attempted to seize the Danish province of Schleswig. Denmark decisively beat back the German assault in 1851, but less than a decade-and-a-half later, the Germans returned, this time with a new set of leaders: the imperially-minded Otto von Bismark; the man who would remake the German army, Helmut von Moltke; and the King of Prussia and future Kaiser of the German Empire, Wilhelm I (Steinberg, 2013. 7. 'I have beaten them all'). This war the German faction won decisively, stripping Denmark of Schleswig and moving the Danish border significantly farther north than it stands today.

Though the border would be adjusted southwards after the World Wars, leading to the modern Danish-German border, the German state is still known as Schleswig-Holstein.

Migration and Industrialization

It is perhaps the long period of domestic peace that prompted Scandinavians to begin emigrating out of the region. Long periods of peace and slow development led to families often not having enough resources, or to sons lacking a proper inheritance. Scandinavians, following trends in other European countries, such as Ireland, Italy, Germany, and eastern Europe, began migrating westwards, particularly to the United States.

The big waves of migration out of Scandinavia began in the 1860s to the 1880s, but didn't seem to taper off until the 1930s. Like immigrants from other parts of Europe, they left their homelands in search of greater economic opportunities. Similar to their Viking ancestors who had the desire for a better life, they found that their best opportunities lay across the sea.

Between 1820 and 1920, a century which saw vast expansion, growth, and development on both sides of the Atlantic, just over two million people from the Nordic countries settled in the United States (Danish Immigrants, n.d.). Some 80% of these migrants came from Norway, while Denmark saw the fewest number of migrants (possibly owing to the early start of industrialization in Copenhagen, which increased economic opportunities for locals. Norway did not see a similar development until much later).

These new migrants did not settle where their ancestors did in Newfoundland and in the Delaware River Valley, but collected in large settlements, rather famously in Minnesota and neighboring American states and Canadian provinces. There was no watershed moment for Minnesota to be chosen as a hub of Scandinavian migration, with many locals saying "Well, it's cold here too!" as if to explain this demographic transition. Though the truth is more banal: Scandinavians were looking for economic opportunity, and Minnesota happened to have it at the time that they were looking.

The Swedish author Frederika Bremer journeyed to the region in 1850 and wrote letters back to her homeland, later published in a book. She wrote, "This Minnesota is a glorious country, and just the country for northern emigrants. Just the country for a new Scandinavia" (Roper, 2022). And like most other locations where migrant communities gather, once they are established, they begin to attract others from the homeland who like familiar faces, languages, foods, and environments. Minnesota maintains Nordic heritage like a badge of honor, and its (generally) progressive politics are an interesting indicator of a cultural connection with their homeland long after the people have become culturally, politically, and emotionally Americans.

As mentioned, however, it is possible that Denmark saw the lowest number of migrants because they were both expanding into their own new territories (Greenland, mainly) and also were expanding economic opportunities with the industrialization of Copenhagen. The Industrial Revolution would lag behind their neighbors in Germany, France, and Britain in particular, but it had come to Scandinavia, and with it new economic opportunities.

The tapering off of migration to the Americas and its eventual decline in the 1930s, when industrialization peaked in pre-war Scandinavia, points to the emigration being fueled by a lack of these economic opportunities. As soon as Scandinavians saw new opportunities in their own homeland—building railroads, working in factories, opening new shops—they no longer felt the call to adventure across the old whale roads of their ancestors, and now cousins.

Some still did, of course.

The Exploration of Greenland

Since the Viking colonies of Greenland were abandoned in the 1400s, Greenland had undergone a series of demographic changes. Those known to the Danes as the Thule people but referred to more broadly as the proto-Inuit began to sail the icy seas between (what is today) the Canadian Arctic Archipelago, and hunted and fished the seas around Greenland (Nationalmuseet i København, n.d.). As the Norse colonies waned, the Thule expanded. Better adapted to the subsistence hunting and gathering that the Norse were not fond of at that point in history, the Thule seemed to thrive in the absence of the Vikings and became the dominant cultural group on Greenland after the failure of the Viking colonies (Grey, 2014).

Despite the lack of any semblance of territorial control over the island, Danish kings maintained for generations that they were still very much the rightful kings of Greenland. Not that anyone seemed to challenge that idea, even the Thule people, who didn't seem completely aware of their new homeland's history.

In the 1600s, Danish Kings began to renew interest in the territory, but it wasn't until the 1700s that expeditions were dispatched to locate the site of the abandoned colonies, and to establish the seeds of new ones (Parker, 2015. Chapter 5). In 1721, Christian missionaries established Godthåb, which would later grow into the Greenlandic capital Nuuk (Barraclough, 2019). As often happened, however, in the mixing of Europe and the New World, Europeans spread smallpox among the local Thule community, and a large portion of the non-European population of Greenland was killed by disease shortly after (Waples et al., 2021).

The Congress of Vienna stripped Norway from Danish governance, but the overseas possessions—in the Caribbean, on the West African coast, and in the North and Norwegian Seas—remained under Copenhagen's jurisdiction.

Danish exploration and control over Greenland steadily expanded throughout the 19th Century. But in the era of empire, lands as remote and inhospitable as Greenland, Tibet, the deepest parts of Africa, the most unreachable islands in the Pacific, and the frozen continent of Antarctica all attracted rivals for territory, national pride, scientific discovery, and personal achievement.

The United States, though relatively late to

the game of Empire, had made its own bid for exploration and conquest of the Arctic. Robert E. Peary, an officer in the US Navy, conducted multiple expeditions across the Arctic circle, including through Greenlandic territory (Koch, 1925). The United States, like all other Western powers, were happy to acknowledge Danish sovereignty over the entire island of Greenland, but when Peary journeyed north, he found a few anomalies not found on his maps, and so claimed them as islands in the name of the United States. The largest and most notable of these was Peary Island, "discovered" on Peary's 1891–2 expedition (ibid.).

The Danish government was none too pleased to have this American encroachment on their territory, but was certainly not powerful enough to resist the American military, which was growing in strength and power. Their only hope was to force the Americans to recognize that Peary Island didn't exist.

A tall order, but the Danish gambit succeeded. A number of expeditions were dispatched to figure out if Peary Island in fact existed, or if it was attached to the Greenland mainland. Ejnar Mikkelsen and his teammate Iver P. Iversen, in a harrowing journey where they both nearly lost their lives on multiple occasions, recovered key maps and notes from Mylius Erichsen, who died of exposure after charting how and where Peary "Island" connected to Greenland. Mikkelsen brought the notebooks and maps back to Denmark in 1910. And in 1912, another Danish explorer, Knud Rasmussen, used those maps to look at the region himself and confirm that the Peary Channel did not exist (see Mikkelsen, 2003).

After this was proven, the United States recognized Peary Island as Peary Land, which was adjoined to Greenland, and therefore under exclusively Danish jurisdiction.

Three New Nations

When Scandinavia emerged into the 20th Century, it was as a divided region. Finland was a vassal of the Russian Empire. Norway was in an unequal relationship with their dominant partner, Sweden. Denmark, though their experiment in a colonial empire had mostly failed, maintained control over Iceland and Greenland, control which continued to expand for some time. But it was not to last.

The first of the nations to emerge was Norway. Norway was held as an appendage to the Kingdom of Sweden after the Congress of Vienna. This was frustrating, as there were nationalistic forces hoping for an independent

Kingdom of Norway, now thrust back under foreign control. However, to placate those independence-minded Norwegians, the Swedish powers essentially resurrected the old idea of the Kalmar Union to Norway: Norway would still exist as a separate kingdom and legal entity as Sweden (just as it did in the Kalmar era), but the (completely separate) title King of Norway would just happen to rest on the head of the reigning King of Sweden.

This arrangement worked for about a century. But as the 20th Century dawned, and nationalism took on new forms across all of Europe, the idea for a resurrected Kingdom of Norway took hold once more.

Once a proud nation with kings of its own, Norway had felt for decades, if not centuries, that it had become a territorial prize to be won by either Denmark or Sweden. Some 15 and 20 wars had been fought between the two, often resulting in Norway changing hands (Grey, 2015). But no longer. They were a nation, and a people who sought their own destiny and sovereignty.

The Norwegian legislature voted on the 7th of June, 1905 to be an independent nation (Elloway, 2013. Nationalism & Identity). This escalation of the situation threatened war. After all, all Stockholm had to do to deny it was to simply... ignore the declaration and send in their military to stop any further organizing for independence, leading to a destabilization of the region at a bad time to have instability (see World War I, just a mere nine years away). Deciding to resolve the issue, the Swedish King Oscar II abdicated his claim to the throne of Norway (The Editors of Encyclopaedia Britannica, 1998b). This effectively ended the personal union known as the United Kingdoms of Sweden and Norway, and made Norway an independent state. The Norwegian legislature elected a new king, the Danish Prince Carl, who took the throne as King Haakon VII (The Royal House of Norway, n.d.). His grandson, King Olaf, sits on the throne of Norway to this day.

It was Finland next that would achieve independence. Albeit whereas Norway achieved a peaceful independence, very much avoiding war, Finland would emerge after the most devastating conflict in Europe up to that point in time.

World War I began in the autumn of 1914, and in the trenches of France and Belgium, across the plains of Poland, Belarus, and Russia, in the oil fields of Romania, and against the U-boat torpedoes in the North Sea, millions of

Europeans were killed in the conflict. An unintentional result of this was that the Russian Empire collapsed, and in its place was an even bloodier conflict, the Russian Civil War, which ended with the rise of a Communist regime: the Soviet Union.

The powers of Western Europe were eager to have this frightening entity (from their perspective) as literally far away as possible. Additionally, the lessons of the nationalistic 19th Century had been passed on to peoples in Eastern Europe who now cried out for their own nations. In 1920, after the signing of the Treaty of Versailles, though it would be some time before their borders had been drawn or stabilized, new countries littered the maps of Europe: Poland, Czechoslovakia, Austria, Hungary, Yugoslavia, Estonia, Latvia, Lithuania, and, of course, Finland.

Finnish independence predates the Versailles Treaty (of course, they were there at Versailles to promote their interests as a state) and started in 1917, as Finland was worried that the Bolshevik Revolution would spread to Finland if they didn't find ways to insulate themselves (Maavara, n.d.). In 1917, the Finnish legislature declared independence from Russia. It almost immediately triggered a civil war, as there were many in Finland who saw the Bolsheviks as inspirational, and a model for what could be done in Finland to establish a revolutionary state. The most conservative of Finns were interested in going the other direction, and inviting a German prince over to take over the role as the new King of Finland (Foley, 2020). Neither idea won out. The Communist revolution would not take root in Finland, and by the time the Versailles Treaty was signed, Finland was and would remain a republic.

Iceland, much like Finland, was always on the fringe of the Nordic world. Iceland was treated much as a colony would be, with a culture that had diverged from the "homeland" and a language that was closer to the language of their Viking settlers than the native language of Denmark (Haraldsdottir, 2019). In 1874, this led to the establishment of "home rule" in Iceland, effectively making it an autonomous region in the Kingdom of Denmark. In 1918, Danish and Icelandic authorities signed the "Act of Union" in which Iceland was formally recognized as an independent Kingdom (Kristinsson, 2000). But like the Kalmar Union of the late medieval period, and the Swedish Empire with its very own Kingdom of Norway through the 19th Century, Iceland was an independent nation, but tied to Denmark through a personal union with the Danish monarchy.

The Nazis invaded Denmark on 9 April 1940. A month later on 10 May 1940, British forces landed in Reykjavik and began the Allied occupation of Iceland to preempt a German flank across the Norwegian Sea (Greenfield et al., 1958/1990, Chapter 3). Iceland was eager to maintain complete neutrality of their small country, so the British turned over administration to the neutral United States. The US entered the war in 1941, and on 17 June 1944 the Icelandic Althing voted to abolish the monarchy and become a full republic (Office of the Historian, Foreign Service Institute, n.d.).

The Second World War

Scandinavia, as a whole, played a relatively small role in the Second World War, and not in any unified sense. This section will go over, in brief, how the War affected the four countries of mainland Scandinavia.

Nazi Germany crossed its northern border at 4:00 a.m. in the morning of April 9, 1940, twenty minutes later, German paratroopers had landed in Copenhagen (Thomas, 2014). The German Luftwaffe (Air Force) destroyed the small Danish air force while it sat on the tarmac, and within six hours, the Danish government was under complete Nazi control. It was German blitzkrieg (lightning war) tactics at their most potent, and was the shortest campaign that the Germany military would conduct in the entire war.

Though the Danish campaign would be the shortest that the German military would undertake in the entire war, Operation Weserübung wasn't over. Nazi Germany, bent on (if not world, then) European domination, immediately continued their campaign into Norway. The campaign would last another two months, owing partly to the vastly larger size of Norway to solidify control (Nilesh, 2012).

It was here that one of the most infamous men of the War (among a long list of infamous men during that era) took the stage. Vidkun Quisling was a former defense minister to the Kingdom of Norway, who had taken a hard right turn in politics and founded his own fascist movement, Nasjonal Samling, though failed to achieve even modest electoral success. When the Nazis invaded Oslo, Quisling went onto the radio to announce his support of the invasion, and attempted (via the radio) a coup d'etat in support of his own party's control of Norway joining the Axis (Albert, 2023).

The Nazis placed control of Norway under the Reichskommissariat Norwegen. Like most places under the German military government, they also set out to establish a civilian puppet regime that would ultimately take over once the war was won. Quisling's regime was personally recognized by Hitler himself within 24 hours of the occupation of Oslo. Quisling's government would remain in power until 8 May 1945—in other words, for virtually the entirety of World War II, until the unconditional surrender of Nazi Germany (Dahl, 1999. p. 365). Quisling surrendered, knowing that after the capitulation of Germany, Norway would follow in no time. He was held captive by Allied Norwegian forces, tried for his crimes, and executed on the 24th of October, 1945. To this day, Quisling is a term, common across Europe, for a traitor, much as Benedict Arnold is used as shorthand for a traitor in American English (United States Holocaust Memorial Museum, 2021b).

Moving eastwards, Sweden was, like Iceland, technically neutral, though it was essentially trapped from without and within by fascist forces, and if Sweden presented a hardline of resistance against pro-German factions, it could have found itself in a precarious situation. Prior to the War, race pseudoscience and ideas about Aryan and Nordic racial superiority were all the rage across northern Europe, and Sweden was no exception (Melander, 2021). Many, including the Swedish explorer Sven Hedin, mixed these ideas of racial superiority with colonial expansionist mindsets, religious mysticism, and fascist apologia (DER SPIEGEL 4/1949, 1949). Hedin, who was famous for exploring across Asia generally and Tibet in particular, not only met Hitler in a propaganda stunt that profited the Nazi war machine very well, he also started praising Hitler and blaming the Allies for the outbreak of war in some of his later writings (Ryback, 2010. p. 218).

Less well-connected and wealthy Swedes with fascist leanings, disappointed that their country resisted joining the Axis powers, took a different route. As we will discuss below, when the Soviet Union invaded Finland in the Winter War, Finland asked for aid from Sweden. Resisting being drawn directly into the conflict, Sweden declared itself a non-combatant, crucially distinct from being neutral. Sweden would send no soldiers to aid Finland's fight, but was happy to let Swedish volunteers travel across the Baltic if they wanted to support the Finnish defense against Communism (Egorov, 2020). Some 8,000 Swedes volunteered to fight on the Finnish front, and the Swedish government sent hundreds of thousands of weapons: mostly small arms, but also field guns, artillery, vehicles, and even aircraft, some of which were flown by Swedish pilots (Wangel, 1982. p. 136).

Just as Iceland was a technically neutral nation essential to the Allies, so Sweden was a technically neutral nation essential to the Axis. The rail lines that criss-crossed Sweden were put to use by Axis forces, and Swedish iron ore was essential to the German war effort. Though this does not tell the full story. After the fall of Norway, thousands of Norwegians fled the Quisling government to Sweden. They began preparing to take back their homeland by force. The Swedish government tried to pass themselves off as helping these Norwegians by saying they were training future Norwegian police officers (Beck, 2021. p. 345).

It is also worth noting that while Sweden had a fascist-friendly population, and Swedish manpower and resources helped parts of the fascist war effort, Sweden, though friendly to fascism like Spain, was also, like Spain, a refuge for Jews fleeing the reach of the Holocaust (Koblik, 1984). Hedin, the explorer of Tibet who met personally with Hitler and wrote favorably of the Nazi regime, was also openly critical of aspects of National Socialism that he found disfavorable. Indeed, in 1937, Germany refused to publish his book Germany and World Peace because Hedin pulled no punches when it came to criticizing the stark antisemitism of the Nazi regime (Mehmel, n.d.). Hedin himself lobbied in favor of Jews fleeing to Sweden for safety, as well as the Norwegians who escaped the SS in their homeland. The full story of World War II in Sweden is one that only serves to get more twisted and complicated, but we must move further east.

Much as Napoleon and Alexander divided Europe between a western sphere and an eastern one, so Hitler and Stalin did the same at the conclusion of the Spanish Civil War in 1939. The Molotov-Ribbentrop Pact divided Europe into a Hitlerian West and a Stalinist East, with Berlin and Moscow agreeing to partition Poland between them (Zamoyski, 2009. TWENTY. War). On 1 September 1939, the German Wehrmacht flowed into Poland from the west, and the Soviet Red Army from the east. Poland held out as long as it could, but ultimately fell. Stalin, for whatever reason, trusted Hitler, and so sought to consolidate his new empire. After Poland, the Red Army marched into Lithuania, Latvia, Estonia, and then Finland (Snyder, 2012. Chapter 5).

Stalin expected only token resistance, and for Finland to fall quickly and be absorbed into the Soviet empire. The Finnish SSR was inaugurated and songs were commissioned for the victory parade in Red Square (Edwards, 2006. p. 272). All of it would go to waste. The Finns put up fierce resistance. The struggle between Finland and the Soviet Union became known as the Winter War and was a complete disaster for the USSR. While the official figures were doctored to reflect less poorly on the Red Army, estimates of Soviet casualties range from 450,000 to over a million (Krivosheev, 1997).

The Finns, however, suffered a total of 70,000 casualties, a fraction of what their aggressors lost (Nenye et al., 2018). The defense of their homeland took just over three months, ending on March 13, 1940, with Finland only making minor territorial concessions to the USSR's most northwestern provinces. The event exposed the terrible disorganization then current in the Red Army, and highlighted how ill-prepared the Soviet Union was for war with a prepared power, as well as the failure of the western Allies (Britain and France, primarily) to respond to the deepening crisis in eastern Europe (Reese, 2008).

Finally, it is worth discussing one

Scandinavian History

Scandinavian of particular note in World War II: Raoul Wallenberg. Wallenberg was born in 1912 near Stockholm. He wanted to become an architect, but became increasingly political (primarily anti-Nazi) as war engulfed the continent. He and his sister were invited to a private screening of "Pimpernel" Smith, a British film made as anti-Nazi propaganda. He eventually made his way to Hungary, walking into the Swedish embassy in Budapest on July 9th, 1944 (Marton, 2002).

The summer of 1944 was one of the deadliest in Europe's history. Operation Barbarossa, the Nazi invasion of the USSR, was in full swing. The western Allies had landed in northern France, and were marching (and bombing) across Italy. The partisan operations taking place in the Balkans were to have bloody consequences for decades. And to hurry along their ideological goal of a racially pure Europe, the Nazis encouraged their puppet regimes across Europe to deport their Jewish citizens to extermination camps. Wallenberg, who was essentially a volunteer at the Swedish embassy, made it his mission to ensure that Budapest's Jewish citizens would not go.

Wallenberg's actions in Budapest are too numerous to go into in full here, but a few examples will be given (see Evans, 2018). Wallenberg ran an extensive espionage network dedicated solely to saving the lives of Hungarian Jews. When he got word of a coming raid, he would do things like erect a Swedish flag in front of their door, and install signs that read "The Swedish Library" or "The Swedish Research Institute." These efforts saved some 10,000 people. He also developed fake, yet official-looking, passports filled with stamps (to appear well-used) that he issued to get some of his beneficiaries to safety in Sweden (if they could find passage). In one notable incident, he stood in front of a train wearing a similarly fake-yet-official-looking uniform that was bound for Auschwitz (United States Holocaust Memorial Museum, 2021a). He then climbed on top of the train and handed out his fake passports. In another incident, one where Nazi officers had pulled Hungarian Jews to the Danube, where they tied them together and shot one (in a bizarre effort to save bullets) so the weight of the dead body would drag and drown the survivors, Wallenberg, in perhaps one of his most dangerous actions, went to the riverbank of the Danube where the massacre had begun and began shouting at the soldiers, ordering them to stop.

With nothing more than his prime Aryan

looks, a fake uniform, and conviction, Raoul Wallenberg, at only 32, is largely credited with the survival of a Jewish community in Budapest (Levine, 2010). His deeds are worthy of so many noble songs and sagas, much like his Viking ancestors. But in true Viking fashion, where pillaging and conquering often resulted in a crown, Wallenberg's efforts in defense of a far-flung community he had neither familial, ethnic, nor religious connection with were rewarded with imprisonment and murder. Somewhat ironically, not even by the Nazis.

The tide of war on the eastern front turned after the Battle of Stalingrad in February 1943. The Red Army swept across eastern Europe (but not Finland) all the way into Berlin and Vienna, and, of course, Budapest. Wallenberg's fake credentials, passports, and uniforms at that point worked against him. The Soviets were not fooled, and suspected him of being a spy, either of the SS or of the United States. He voluntarily went to the Soviet commander to answer these accusations of espionage on January 17, 1945. Though many theories exist, including one that he died of a heart attack in a gulag in 1957, he was never seen again (see Matz, 2019).

The Cold War

Just as the relationship between Napoleon

and Alexander led to an invasion of Russia, the failure of the dictator, and the reordering of the world with a large Russian sphere of influence, history very much repeated itself after World War II. Germany was divided down the middle, with much of eastern Europe either outright annexed into the Soviet Union (the Baltics, a large eastern swath of Poland, and all of Ukraine) or with pro-Soviet regimes in power (Poland, East Germany, Hungary, Romania, Bulgaria, and briefly Yugoslavia). Meanwhile, the western Allies were eager to hold onto Iceland, liberate Denmark and Norway, and sway Sweden and Finland to their side.

The most notable development in the international history of Scandinavia at this point was the development of the North Atlantic Treaty Organization (NATO), a defense pact the western Allies developed to protect themselves from the potential for a Soviet pre-emptive strike. The United States, Britain, and France were the big partners in the alliance, with Iceland, Denmark, and Norway joining as founding members. The effects of this development resonate deeply in the 21st Century, with both Sweden and Finland applying to join NATO after the Russian invasion in February 2022 (NATO, 2023).

The other political development in this period was the process of "Finlandization," a term which has come to be generally derogatory in international politics, but in Finland was determined to be a practical measure to prevent further disaster.

The Soviet Army was prepared for the disorganized and two-front war waged in Poland in 1939, but, owing to the small and determined Finns, was unable to achieve more than minor victories with major casualties. Yet the tide turned after Stalingrad pointed out to Finland that a well-organized, well-armed Soviet Union could easily stamp out the Finnish state and return them to a Communist version of the Grand Duchy of Finland in a new Russian empire (Walker, 2001).

Before the establishment of NATO in 1949, Finland had few defensive options in terms of resisting Soviet political and military domination. And Stalin proved that he was willing to probe for weaknesses in the western defensive line: Berlin, Greece, Iran, China, and Korea would all take center stage in Soviet or pro-Soviet campaigns to try to test the weaknesses of the pre-NATO western allies (compare with how the fascists from Germany, Italy, and Japan were able to gauge the disorder in western diplomacy as they marched through China, Ethiopia, Czechoslovakia, and Poland, and then how Finland eventually swayed them to their side).

This was how Finland began to adopt policies that were acquiescent to the USSR. Officially, the policy in Finland was called the Paasikivi doctrine, developed by Finnish President Juho Paasikivi. The policy emphasized the need to remain passive towards the USSR and develop a relationship built on mutual trust (The Editors of Encyclopaedia Britannica, 1999).

In practice, this developed into a Finland that was not allied to the western powers by any means. In fact, the Soviet Union made sure to pressure Finland into adopting a policy that said they would resist influence from "Germany or its allies," and that if they were invaded, they would be required to request Soviet military assistance. As a partial consequence for acquiescing so readily to Soviet demands out of an instinct of survival, Finland did not get any funds from the US-based Marshall Plan to rebuild Europe after World War II (Rupasov, 2018). (Thankfully, Finland did not face nearly as complete levels of destruction as Germany, France, or Italy.)

Iceland and Greenland in the Cold War went from being outskirts of the Scandinavian world, to crucial outposts of the western alliance. No longer bound by longboats and wind-blown sails, at the heart of the Cold War was the threat of nuclear war: driven by land-based missiles, bombs dropped from long-range bombers, and nuclear-tipped missiles launched from submarines. The USA and USSR were able to stare at each other most efficiently (without European or Asian intermediaries) over the Arctic Circle, and so the western (American) hold on Greenland and Iceland held that these were crucial, strategic points on the map, and continues to hold in the 21st Century (Sasgen, 2009).

The development, leasing, and expansion of NATO bases primarily operated by the United States has been a point of contention between the United States, its allied governments, and the locals who live in those areas, including Icelanders and native Greenlanders, since the beginning of the Cold War. One incident in particular highlights not only the careless danger of Cold War technology, but its active danger to the lives of locals: the Thule Air Base B-52 Crash of 1968.

Thule Air Base, named after the native

inhabitants of Greenland who moved onto the island after(/during) the failure of the Viking Colonies, was ratified as a strategic NATO point in 1951 (Rhode, 2019). It was important for monitoring Soviet naval activity across the Arctic Ocean. It was expanded often to accommodate further operations through the '60s, and became a forwarding base for nuclear bombers, including the B-52, the successor to the B-29 that dropped the first atomic bombs on Hiroshima and Nagasaki.

In the incident, a B-52 armed with both conventional and nuclear weapons experienced a cabin fire on 21 January 1968. The six-person crew abandoned the craft, with one dying when their ejection seat failed. The plane then continued to fly until it crashed into sea ice in the Baffin Bay. The non-nuclear explosives on the craft exploded. While the "weak link" safeties on the nuclear weapons prevented the worst from happening, the damage to the bombs' containers caused a catastrophic leak and contamination (Taschner, 1968).

The incident led to a massive clean-up operation, and widespread political opposition to NATO policies, including policies of non-disclosure. Denmark, which was the governing authority in Greenland, had adopted a policy of a nuclear-free zone in 1957 (Jorgensen, 2018). The Thule Incident revealed that either Danish leaders had lied, or that NATO or the United States had decided to override Danish and Greenlandic sovereignty.

The complexities of the Thule Incident are vast, and too much to get along here. What it does go to show is that even the most outer fringes of Scandinavia, well into the 20th Century, remained intertwined with some of the most fundamental developments of the world, including the development of nuclear technologies, the complexity of Cold War diplomacy and espionage, and the challenges of global war..

CONCLUSION

The Vikings have enticed the cultural imagination since the Romantic period. The Ride of the Valkyries remains one of Wagner's most well-known and recognized operas, even to the modern day, and serves as both a celebration of Nordic heritage, and served as a call to action for 20th Century Nationalists.

Since then the Vikings have served as inspiration for fantastic worlds and journeys. Philologist and linguist J.R.R. Tolkien originally set out to make a translation of the Finnish national epic, the Kalavela, until he decided to redefine the fantasy genre with The Hobbit, The Lord of the Rings, and The Silmarillion. Other than taking inspiration from Norse mythology regarding the "light elves" of Aelfheim, he also lifted the Nordic runes for use in his Dwarven alphabet, recreated the tale of Beowulf set in his Middle Earth (itself a name taken from the Norse Midgard), and entirely lifted the lineage of the Dwarven Kings to represent his own Dwarven royalty. Long after Tolkien's death, the designers who worked on Peter Jackson's film adaptation took further inspiration from Nordic artifacts to create a unique aesthetic for the Kingdom of Rohan.

The sagas of the Vikings have made their way into movies, TV shows, and video games, lifted in fictional form from ancient manuscripts and retold to modern media. The 1999 video game Age of Empires II: The Age of Kings depicted a scenario called Vinlandsaga, where unnamed Vikings travel from Iceland and fight their way through hostile Greenlanders (a significant creative license), all with the goal of settling Vinland while being attacked by hostile Skraelings. The 2017 game Hellblade: Senua's Sacrifice tells the story of a Pictish warrior who fights her way through a nightmarish dreamscape filled with terrifying Vikings who invaded Senua's Celtic island home to kill her people, burn her village, and turn her lover in a "blood eagle" sacrifice. As a result, the player has to guide Senua through Helheim to fight Surtr; Valravn, the Norse god of illusion; Fenrir; and ultimately Hel herself, to set her lover's soul to rest.

But even when the vast imaginary mythos of Nordic mythology is too limiting for creators, fantasy authors have taken a page out of Tolkien's book and used the Vikings as inspiration for characters and settings for their own worlds. Polish author Andrzej Sapkowski used the pagan Norse as inspiration for his Skellige Isles, depicted in both The Witcher books and video games. In George R.R. Martin's A Song of Ice and Fire, and the TV show Game of Thrones, the Iron Islands draw their culture of sailing, raiding, and an obsession with salt water and the sea from Viking history. The perennial classic video game The Elder Scrolls V: Skyrim takes place in a vast fictional universe, a continent called Tamriel, while the Skyrim installment of the series takes place almost entirely in a country that is less inspired by Norse mythology, and more a fantastic reimagining of it. The people who inhabit the country are even referred to as "Nords."

In an inspiring twist, the Grishaverse, a series of novels by Leigh Bardugo, and a 2021 TV show named after the first book Shadow and Bone, imagines a fantasy version of Russia, called Ravka, bordered by a fantasy reimagining of China to the south, called Shu Han, and a fantasy reimagining of Sweden during the reign of Charles XII, called Fjerda, actively fighting their version of the Great Northern War (but with magic).

Author Eric Flint saw much to be inspired about the Swedish Empire when he wrote 1632, about a small American town in West Virginia which is thrown back in time and space to Germany in the middle of the Thirty Years' War. The story's main non-fictional character is none other than King Gustav II, who transformed the modern world, saw Sweden's expansion, and greatly contributed to the survival of Protestantism in Europe. Flint's own analysis of the man is in the middle of his time travel/alternate history novel (Flint, 2000. Chapter 34):

In the centuries to come, they would call Gustavus Adolphus the Father of Modern War. Then they would take to quarreling over it. For he wasn't, really. That title, if it can be given to anyone, more properly belongs to Maurice of Nassau.

Flint then goes on to elaborate on the many ways Gustav II's "contributions" to modern warfare were really only the collation and use of strategies that predated him, and he was most able to put to effective use by combining them in good strategy and tactics.

Flint prefers a different title for Gustav II:

The Father of Modern War, Gustavus Adolphus almost certainly was not. But he may very well have been the Father of the Modern World. Because then, at that place [Breitenfeld], at the moment when the Saxons broke and the Inquisition bade fair to triumph over all of Europe, the king of Sweden stood his ground.

Scandinavia, first as the decentralized Vikings spreading across the continent of Europe and the seas of the north, had their vibrant place in the sun. A few centuries later, that place would be resurrected and taken by one of their successors: the Swedes, who began as a rebel kingdom, and rose to become an empire that toppled crowns and thrones, and in whose ashes the Russian Empire emerged, a historic consequence which has obvious echoes in the world as late as the 21st Century.

In February of 2022, the army of the Russian Federation crossed into Ukraine in an attempt to "liberate" (i.e. conquer) provinces that they deemed were theirs, to extinguish the idea that Ukrainian culture was distinct from Russian culture, and to enforce (if not outright declare) that the Russian Empire was still alive and well. Ukraine responded not only with force, but with a short propaganda campaign of their own, trying to remind the world that Kyiv (settled first as a Viking trading post) predates Moscow, as does the Kingdom that rose up around it, Kyivan Rus'. Even the symbolism of the original Scandinavian inhabitants of the land is still seen on the national seal of Ukraine: an ornate cross section of a Viking ship, once the symbol of Rurik, the first king of Kyivan Rus'. Even the name of the aggressive party in this story, Russia, comes from a word denoting the Viking settlers.

And though all of that is ancient history, the fall of Sweden led to the rise of Russia, the rise of Russia led to their dominion in western European politics in the Napoleonic and post-Napoleonic worlds, the eventual fall of the Russian Empire to the Bolsheviks in 1917, the rise of the Soviet Union, the devastation of World War II, the Soviet-empire of the Cold War era that extended as far as the Elbe, the eventual collapse of the Soviet Union, the rise of KGB agent Vladimir Putin to his current perch over the Soviet apocalyptic state, and our current state of world affairs.

Closer to home, the mythology of Scandinavia is

still vibrantly alive and active. While Norse and Scandinavian history serve as fresh raw material for books, movies, TV shows, and video games, modern Scandinavian society has gathered a sort of mythology about itself that is reflected in the hopes and dreams of Western progressives and economic migrants and political refugees from the developing world.

Scandinavia remains one of the most popular destinations for refugees from the Middle East and Africa. And though three Scandinavian countries still retain monarchs on their thrones, they are also vibrant progressive democracies, with Finland and Iceland, the two republics on the fringe of the Scandinavian world, being two of the freest and most democratic countries in the world, with progressive social policies and extremely egalitarian cultures. This is most likely why, in addition to their relatively safe cultures and societies, they are also a source of inspiration for social democrats and progressive policy makers across the Western world.

REFERENCES

Adams, M. (2019). *The Viking Wars : War and Peace in King Alfred's Britain, 789-955.* Pegasus Books.

The Age of Enlightenment - Finland. (n.d.). Www.spottinghistory.com. Retrieved February 13, 2023, from https://www.spottinghistory.com/historicalperiod/age-of-enlightenment-finland/

Albert, D. (2023, January 4). *Norway's Traitor: The Story of Vidkun Quisling.* Life in Norway. https://www.lifeinnorway.net/vidkun-quisling/

Alcuin. (1974). *Alcuin of York, C. A.D. 732 to 804* (S. Allott, Ed.).

Aldhouse-Green, M. J. (2015). *Bog Bodies Uncovered : Solving Europe's Ancient Mystery.* Thames & Hudson.

ÁrnasonJ. (1866). *Icelandic Legends* (G. E. J. Powell & E. Magnússon, Trans.). London, Longmans, Green & Co.

Arnórsdóttir, A. (2019, September 11). *History of Iceland, 1840s to the Second World War.* Nordics.info. https://nordics.info/show/artikel/history-of-iceland-1840s-to-the-second-world-war/

Asbridge, T. S. (2009). *The Crusades: The Authoritative History of the War for the Holy Land.* HarperCollins.

Ashby, S. P. (2015). What really caused the Viking Age? The social content of raiding and exploration. *Archaeological Dialogues, 22*(01), 89–106. https://doi.org/10.1017/s1380203815000112

Bain, R. N. (1911). *Charles X. (King of Sweden).* Wikisource.org; Wikimedia Foundation, Inc. https://en.wikisource.org/wiki/1911_Encyclop%C3

%A6dia_Britannica/Charles_X._(King_of_Sweden) Originally published by Encyclopædia Britannica c. 1911.

Bakshi, A. (2012). *66° North*. Akhil Bakshi.

Barraclough, E. R. (2019, August 21). *Explore Nuuk: the rainbow capital of Greenland*. HistoryExtra. https://www.historyextra.com/period/viking/explore-city-nuuk-greenland-norse-godthab/

Beck, J. (2021). *Die Gefechte in Norwegen, Band 3*. Jazzybee Verlag.

Blom, F. (2014). Neighbours in America. New Sweden and New Netherland. *Www.academia.edu*. https://www.academia.edu/80285780/Neighbours_in_America_New_Sweden_and_New_Netherland

Bridgeford, A. (2009). *1066: The Hidden History in the Bayeux Tapestry*. Walker Books.

Brimnes, N. (2021, October 29). *The colonialism of Denmark-Norway and its legacies*. Nordics.info; Aarhus University. https://nordics.info/show/artikel/the-colonialism-of-denmark-norway-and-its-legacies

Brown, D. M. (2018, August 3). *The Peach Tree War / A Brief History/Herstory about Peaches & Other Things*. Medium. https://medium.com/mnemosynes-musings/the-peach-tree-war-a-brief-history-herstory-about-peaches-other-things-df4a0ce939c6

Brown, G. S. (2003). *The Norman conquest of Southern Italy and Sicily*. Mcfarland.

Burmeister, S. (2013). Fighting wars, gaining status: on the rise of Germanic elites. In D. Sayer & H. William (Eds.), *Mortuary practices and social identities in the Middle Ages : essays in burial archaeology in honour of Heinrich Härke* (pp. 46–63). Liverpool University Press.

Bursche, A. (2002). Circulation of Roman Coinage in

Northern Europe in Late Antiquity. *Histoire & Mesure*, *XVII*(3/4), 121–141. https://doi.org/10.4000/histoiremesure.886

Cahill, T. (1996). *How the Irish Saved Civilization : The Untold Story of Ireland's Heroic Role from the Fall of Rome to the Rise of Medieval Europe*. Anchor Books, Doubleday.

Carey, W. H. (1907). *The Good Old Days of Honorable John Company*. R. Cambray & Co. https://indianculture.gov.in/flipbook/31937

Carstensen, E. (2010). *Closing the Books: Governor Edward Carstensen on Danish Guinea, 1842-50* (T. Storsveen, Trans.). Sub-Saharan Pub.

Chase, S. (2022, June 10). Canada and Denmark reach settlement over disputed Arctic island, sources say. *The Globe and Mail*. https://www.theglobeandmail.com/politics/article-canada-and-denmark-reach-settlement-over-disputed-arctic-island/

Comnena, A. (2015). *The Alexiad* (E. R. A. Sewter, Trans.). Penguin Books.

Covart, E. (2016, September 16). *New Sweden: A Brief History*. Penn State University Libraries. https://libraries.psu.edu/about/collections/unearthing-past-student-research-pennsylvania-history/new-sweden-brief-history

Dahl, H. F. (1999). *Quisling: A Study in Treachery*. Cambridge University Press.

Danielsson, S. K. (2012). *The Explorer's Roadmap to National-Socialism: Sven Hedin, Geography and the Path to Genocide*. Ashgate.

Danish Immigrants. (n.d.). Spartacus Educational. Retrieved January 1, 2023, from https://www.spartacus-educational.com/USAEdenmark.htm

Dasent, G. W. (Ed.). (1861). *The Story of Burnt Njal*. Www.sacred-Texts.com. https://www.sacred-texts.com/neu/ice/njal/njal098.htm

Der Spiegel 4/1949. (1949, January 21). Kopfschütteln um Sven Hedin. *Der Spiegel*. https://www.spiegel.de/politik/kopfschuetteln-um-sven-hedin-a-0b4fd9d0-0002-0001-0000-000044435379

East India Company, the Board of Control, the India Office, & or other British Government Department. (1869). *ABSTRACT OF LETTERS FROM INDIA 1869* (p. 191). British Library: India Office Records and Private Papers; Qatar Digital Library. https://www.qdl.qa/en/archive/81055/vdc_100136851548.0x000011

The Editors of Encyclopaedia Britannica. (1998a, July 20). *Anjala League | Finnish-Swedish conspiracy | Britannica*. Www.britannica.com. https://www.britannica.com/event/Anjala-League#ref18767

The Editors of Encyclopaedia Britannica. (1998b, July 20). *Oscar II | king of Sweden | Britannica*. Www.britannica.com. https://www.britannica.com/biography/Oscar-II

The Editors of Encyclopaedia Britannica. (1998c, October 19). *Biblical literature - Greek, Hungarian, Italian, and Portuguese translations | Britannica*. Www.britannica.com. https://www.britannica.com/topic/biblical-literature/Greek-Hungarian-Italian-and-Portuguese-translations#ref597516

The Editors of Encyclopaedia Britannica. (1999, July 26). *Finland - The postwar period | Britannica*. Www.britannica.com. https://www.britannica.com/place/Finland/The-postwar-period

Edwards, R. (2006). *White Death: Russia's War on Finland 1939–40*. Orion.

Egorov, B. (2020, April 15). *How Swedes fought for and against the USSR in WWII*. Russia Beyond. https://www.rbth.com/history/332014-how-swedes-fought-against-ussr

Elloway, D. (2013). *The Xenophobe's Guide to the Norwegians*. Xenophobe's Guide.

THE ELVES OF ICELAND. (2019, November 16). Your Friend in Reykjavik. https://yourfriendinreykjavik.com/elves-of-iceland/

Evans, R. (2018, December 25). *Behind the Bastards: Special X-Mas Non-Bastard: Raoul Wallenberg, History's Greatest Hero* (No. 40) [Podcast]. iHeartRadio. https://omny.fm/shows/behind-the-bastards/special-x-mas-non-bastard-raoul-wallenberg-history

Extra Credits. (2016, July 30). *Lindisfarne - An Age Borne in Fire - Extra History*. Www.youtube.com. https://www.youtube.com/watch?v=qc_wCJd9DKw&t=27s

Extra Credits. (2017a, August 19). *Great Northern War - When Sweden Ruled the World - Extra History - #1*. Www.youtube.com.
https://www.youtube.com/watch?v=VyBPAz1H-lU

Extra Credits. (2017b). Great Northern War - A Good Plan - Extra History - #2. In *YouTube*. https://www.youtube.com/watch?v=QCTohrWP-Lo

Extra Credits. (2017c, September 9). *Great Northern War - Young and Violent - Extra History - #3*. Www.youtube.com.
https://www.youtube.com/watch?v=dovxeQEDils

Extra Credits. (2017d). Great Northern War - Clash of Kings - Extra History - #4. In *YouTube*.

https://www.youtube.com/watch?v=M6Oon1XGWRc

Extra Credits. (2017e). Great Northern War - Rise and Fall - Extra History - #5. In *YouTube*. https://www.youtube.com/watch?v=0dPI1PzyWjg

Extra Credits. (2017f, October 7). *Great Northern War - Lies - Extra History*. Www.youtube.com. https://www.youtube.com/watch?v=1hGAdzbef4g&t=373s

Extra Credits. (2018a). The Danelaw - Alfred vs. Guthrum - Extra History - #1. In *YouTube*. https://www.youtube.com/watch?v=_K6P3T0NIjo

Extra Credits. (2018b). The Aesir-Vanir War - Extra Mythology. In *YouTube*. https://www.youtube.com/watch?v=g9TET6YTYrk

Extra Credits. (2018c). The Danelaw - The Fall of Eric Bloodaxe - Extra History - #2. In *YouTube*. https://www.youtube.com/watch?v=MvM3wPGAUjE

Extra Credits. (2018d). Yggdrasil - Nine Worlds of the Norse - Extra Mythology. In *YouTube*. https://www.youtube.com/watch?v=HIL7TAO1cT4

Extra Credits. (2018e). Viking Expansion - The Serpent-Riders - Extra History - #1. In *YouTube*. https://www.youtube.com/watch?v=sxItyrp55g8

Extra Credits. (2018f). Viking Expansion - Rollo the Walker - Extra History - #2 [YouTube Video]. In *YouTube*. https://www.youtube.com/watch?v=IOnjG7ocZmI

Extra Credits. (2018g). Viking Expansion - Ireland - Extra History - #3. In *YouTube*. https://www.youtube.com/watch?v=ms3-rhnbw9U

Extra Credits. (2018h, November 17). *Viking Expansion - The Lands of the Rus - Extra History - #4*. Www.youtube.com.

https://www.youtube.com/watch?v=fhz4Fe25rik

Extra Credits. (2018i). *Viking Expansion - A Song of Ice and Greenland - Extra History - #5*. In *YouTube*. https://www.youtube.com/watch?v=kTB8131aGJo

Extra Credits. (2018j). *Viking Expansion - Wine Land - Extra History - #6*. In *YouTube*. https://www.youtube.com/watch?v=SITsfX15jw0

Extra Credits. (2018k). *Viking Expansion - Lies - Extra History*. In *YouTube*. https://www.youtube.com/watch?v=rAI4zRaNO3I

Fihl, E., & Lillelund, C. (2015). *Danish Era (1620-1845)*. National Museum of Denmark. https://en.natmus.dk/historical-knowledge/historical-knowledge-the-world/asia/india/tranquebar/danish-era-1620-1845/

Flint, E. (2000). *1632*. Baen Books.

Foley, L. (2020, July 15). *Frederick Charles of Hesse-Cassel* (credited as liamfoley63, Ed.). European Royal History. https://europeanroyalhistory.wordpress.com/tag/frederick-charles-of-hesse-cassel/

Frilund, G. (n.d.). *The Union's Last War: The Russian-Swedish war of 1808-09*. Www.napoleon-Series.org. Retrieved February 13, 2023, from https://www.napoleon-series.org/military-info/battles/c_finnish.html

Galeotti, M. (2021). *A Short History Of Russia: How the World's Largest Country Invented Itself, From the Pagans to Putin*. Ebury Press UK.

Gibson, C. (2015). *Empire's Crossroads: A History of the Caribbean from Columbus to the Present Day*. Pan Books.

Greenfield, K. R., Fairchild, B., & Blumenson, M. (1990). *Command Decisions*. Center Of Military History,

United States Army. https://web.archive.org/web/20071230145455/http://www.history.army.mil/books/70-7_0.htm (Original work published 1958)

Grey, C. (2014, July 1). *American Empire*. Www.youtube.com. https://www.youtube.com/watch?v=ASSOQDQvVLU&t=167s

Grey, C. (2015, March 25). *Where is Scandinavia?* Www.youtube.com. https://www.youtube.com/watch?v=TsXMe8H6iyc

Gulløv, H. C. (2004). *Grønlands forhistorie*. Gyldendal A/S.

Gunn, J. (2000). *The Years Without Summer: Tracing A.D. 536 and its Aftermath*. British Archaeological Reports Limited.

Haefeli, E. (2006). The Revolt of the Long Swede: Transatlantic Hopes and Fears on the Delaware, 1669. *Pennsylvania Magazine of History and Biography, 130*(2), 137–180. JSTOR.

Haraldsdottir, R. H. (2019, November 7). *Icelandic Language | The Viking Heritage, Development & Modern Times*. Iceland Travel. https://www.icelandtravel.is/blog/icelandic-language-2/

Harper, D. (n.d.a). Etymology of barbarian. Online Etymology Dictionary. Retrieved February 12, 2023, from https://www.etymonline.com/word/barbarian

Harper, D. (n.d.b). Etymology of lorraine. Online Etymology Dictionary. Retrieved February 12, 2023, from https://www.etymonline.com/word/lorraine

Harper, D. (n.d.c). Etymology of skraeling. Online Etymology Dictionary. Retrieved February 13, 2023, from https://www.etymonline.com/word/skraeling

Harper, D. (n.d.d). Etymology of russia. Online

Etymology Dictionary. Retrieved February 13, 2023, from https://www.etymonline.com/word/russia

Hawes, J. (2018). *The Shortest History of Germany*. Old Street Publishing Ltd.

Heršak, E. (2001). The Origins and Migrations of the Uralic People. *Migracijske I Etnicke Teme, 17*(4), 377–404. https://doaj.org/article/964baa00c2664f9286ffdccca83f74cf

Howarth, D. A. (1986). *1066: The Year of the Conquest*. Penguin.

Jameson, J. F., & Johnson, A. (1912). The Swedish Settlements on the Delaware: Their History and Relation to the Indians, Dutch and English, 1638-1664. *The American Historical Review, 17*(2), 381. https://doi.org/10.2307/1833020

Jarus, O. (2010, December 23). *Did the Scots visit Iceland? New research reveals island inhabited 70 years before Vikings thought to have arrived*. Medievalists.net. https://www.medievalists.net/2010/12/did-the-scots-visit-iceland-new-research-reveals-island-inhabited-70-years-before-vikings-thought-to-have-arrived/

Jennings, F. (1984). *The Ambiguous Iroquois Empire*. New York Norton & Co.

Jörberg, L. (1965). Structural change and economic growth: Sweden in the 19th century. *Economy and History, 8*(1), 3–46. https://doi.org/10.1080/00708852.1965.10418997

Jorgensen, T. J. (2018, January 21). *50 years ago, a U.S. military jet crashed in Greenland – with 4 nuclear bombs on board*. PBS NewsHour. https://www.pbs.org/newshour/world/50-years-ago-a-us-military-jet-crashed-in-greenland-with-4-

nuclear-bombs-on-board

Khalimzoda, I. (2018, August 31). *Finnish silence is a myth - Stereotypes can become a part of an identity.* Jyväskylän Ylioppilaslehti. https://www.jylkkari.fi/2018/08/finnish-silence-is-a-myth/

Killings, D. B. (Ed.). (1823). *The Anglo-Saxon Chronicle* (Rev. J. Ingram & Dr. J. A. Giles, Trans.). Project Gutenberg.

Koblik, S. (1984). SWEDEN'S ATTEMPTS TO AID JEWS, 1939-1945. *Scandinavian Studies, 56*(2), 89–113. JSTOR. https://www.jstor.org/stable/40918381

Koch, L. (1925). The Question of Peary Channel. *Geographical Review, 15*(4), 643. https://doi.org/10.2307/208628

Kristinsson, G. H. (2000). From Home Rule to Sovereignty: The Case of Iceland. In G. Baldacchino & D. Milne (Eds.), *Lessons From the Political Economy of Small Islands: The Resourcefulness of Jurisdiction* (pp. 141–155). Palgrave Macmillan.

Krivosheev, G. (1997). *Soviet Casualties and Combat Losses in the Twentieth Century.* Greenhill Books/Lionel Leventhal.

Kujala, A. (2000). The Breakdown of a Society: Finland in the Great Northern War 1700-1714. *Scandinavian Journal of History, 25*(1-2), 69–86. https://doi.org/10.1080/03468750050115591

Lambert, T. (2021, March 14). *A Brief History of Greenland.* Local Histories. https://localhistories.org/a-brief-history-of-greenland/

Larrington, C. (2014). *The Poetic Edda.* OUP Oxford.

Levine, P. A. (2010). *Raoul Wallenberg in Budapest: Myth, History, and Holocaust.* Mitchell Vallentine.

Lewis, J. J. (2019, November 11). *Who Was Princess Olga*

of Kiev? ThoughtCo. https://www.thoughtco.com/princess-olga-of-kiev-3529733

Lindow, J. (2001). *Norse Mythology : A Guide To The Gods, Heroes, Rituals, And Beliefs.* Oxford University Press.

Lunde, H. O. (2014). *A Warrior Dynasty: The Rise and Fall of Sweden as a Military Superpower 1611-1721.* Casemate.

Maavara, A. (Alec). (n.d.). *Finland Divided.* Finland Divided. https://finlanddivided.wordpress.com/

Macculloch, D. (2010). *Christianity: The First Three Thousand Years.* Viking.

Man, J. (2010). *The Gutenberg Revolution.* Random House.

Marton, K. (2002). *Wallenberg: missing hero.* Little, Brown and Company.

Matz, J. (2019). *Stalin's Double-Edged Game: Soviet Bureaucracy and the Raoul Wallenberg Case, 1945–1952.* Lexington Books.

McLynn, F. (1998). *1066: The Year of Three Battles.* Random House (UK).

Mehmel, A. (n.d.). Sven Hedin und die nationalsozialistische Expansionspolitik. *Zeitschrift Für Religions- Und Geistesgeschichte.*

Melander, E. (2021). *Creating "Us and Them": Racial Propaganda and Right-Wing Voting in Interwar Sweden.* https://ericmelander.com/wp-content/uploads/2021/08/racebiology_210804.pdf

Mikkelsen, E. (2003). *Two Against the Ice: A Classic Arctic Survival Story and a Remarkable Account of Companionship in the Face of Adversity* (M. Michael, Trans.). Steerforth.

Morgan, R. J. (2021, May 27). *Three Hundred Years After It Fell, Historians Still Aren't Sure Why Sweden Built an Empire*. The Startup. https://medium.com/swlh/three-hundred-years-after-it-fell-historians-still-arent-sure-why-sweden-built-an-empire-6df720d8777f

National Historic Site Pennsylvania. (2021, September 21). *Gloria Dei Church National Historic Site (U.S. National Park Service)*. Www.nps.gov. https://www.nps.gov/glde/index.htm

Nationalmuseet i København. (n.d.). *Thule*. Nationalmuseet. Retrieved February 16, 2023, from https://natmus.dk/organisation/forskning-samling-og-bevaring/nyere-tid-og-verdens-kulturer/etnografisk-samling/arktisk-forskning/prehistory-of-greenland/thule/

NATO. (2023, January 8). *Secretary General: Sweden and Finland's NATO membership will make us all safer*. NATO. https://www.nato.int/cps/en/natohq/news_210480.htm

Naylor, D. (2017, April 6). *Nicolaus Copernicus' books digitized - Uppsala University, Sweden*. Www.uu.se. https://www.uu.se/en/news/article/?id=8542&typ=artikel

Nenye, V., Munter, P., Wirtanen, T., & Birks, C. (2018). *Finland at War: The Winter War 1939-40*. Osprey Publishing.

Nilesh, P. (2012). NORWAY AND WORLD WAR II: INVASION, OCCUPATION, LIBERATION. *Proceedings of the Indian History Congress*, *73*, 1117–1124. http://www.jstor.org/stable/44156312

Nilsson, M. P. (1992). *Geschichte der griechischen Religion*. C.H.Beck.

Norwich, J. J. (1998). *Byzantium: The Early Centuries*. Knopf.

Norwich, J. J. (2003). *Byzantium: The Decline and Fall*.

Folio Society.

Nuse, I. P. (2018, January 12). *First Scandinavians came from north and south*. Sciencenordic.com. https://sciencenordic.com/archaeology-forskningno-society--culture/first-scandinavians-came-from-north-and-south/1453083#:~:text=People%20started%20settling%20in%20Scandinavia

Ó HógáinD. (2003). *The Celts : a chronological history*. Boydell.

Office of the Historian, Foreign Service Institute. (n.d.). *Iceland - Countries - Office of the Historian*. History.state.gov. https://history.state.gov/countries/iceland

Orchard, A. (1998). *Dictionary of Norse myth and legend*. Cassell.

Parker, P. (2015). *The Northmen's Fury : A History of the Viking World*. Vintage Books.

Peterson, G. D. (2014). *Warrior Kings of Sweden: The Rise of an Empire in the Sixteenth and Seventeenth Centuries*. McFarland.

Price, T. D. (2015). *Ancient Scandinavia : an archaeological history from the first humans to the Vikings*. Oxford University Press.

Reese, R. R. (2008). Lessons of the Winter War: A Study in the Military Effectiveness of the Red Army, 1939–1940. *The Journal of Military History*, 72(3), 825–852. https://doi.org/10.1353/jmh.0.0004

Rhode, B. (2019). *The GIUK Gap's strategic significance*. The International Institute for Strategic Studies. https://www.iiss.org/~/publication/799791dd-7be1-4484-abfd-05fa3a400889/the-giuk-gaps-strategic-significance.pdf

Richards, J. D. (2005). *The Vikings : a very short introduction*. Oxford University Press.

Rimbert. (1998). *Life of Anskar, the Apostle of the North, 801-865* (C. H. Robinson, Trans.). Fordham University.
https://sourcebooks.fordham.edu/basis/anskar.asp

Rodgers, N. (2009). *Ireland, slavery and anti-slavery, 1612-1865*. Palgrave Macmillan.

Roper, E. (2022, May 20). *Why did Scandinavian immigrants choose Minnesota?* Star Tribune. https://www.startribune.com/swedish-norwegian-immigration-minnesota-scandinavian/600174976/

The Royal House of Norway. (n.d.). *King Haakon and Queen Maud*. Www.royalcourt.no. Retrieved February 17, 2023, from https://www.royalcourt.no/seksjon.html?tid=102868&sek=27269

Rupasov, A. I. (2018). USSR and the Compelled Refusal of Finland on the Marshall Plan. *Modern History of Russia*, *8*(4).
https://doi.org/10.21638/11701/spbu24.2018.410

Ryback, T. W. (2010). *Hitler's Private Library: The Books that Shaped His Life*. Vintage Books.

Sasgen, P. T. (2009). *Stalking the Red Bear: The True Story of a U.S. Cold War Submarine's Covert Operations Against the Soviet Union*. St. Martin's Press.

Scott, H. (2011). The Seven Years War and Europe's Ancien Régime. *War in History*, *18*(4), 419–455. https://doi.org/10.1177/0968344511416718

Sienkiewicz, H. (2017). *Delphi Complete Works of Henryk Sienkiewicz (Illustrated)*. Delphi Classics.

Smith, E. W. (2018). *The Echo of Odin: Norse Mythology and Human Consciousness*. Jefferson, North Carolina Mcfarland Et Company, Inc., Publishers.

Smith, K. N. (2018, November 30). *Everything We Know About The Isolated Sentinelese People Of North*

Sentinel Island. Forbes. https://www.forbes.com/sites/kionasmith/2018/11/30/everything-we-know-about-the-isolated-sentinelese-people-of-north-sentinel-island/?sh=1b7c86a935a0

Snyder, T. (2012). *Bloodlands: Europe between Hitler and Stalin*. Basic Books, , Cop.

Solomon, L. (2021, February 1). *The History of the Log Cabin*. The Great Lodge. https://www.greatlodge.ca/post/the-history-of-the-log-cabin

Sprinchorn, C. K. S., Keen, G. B., & Stuyvesant, P. (1884). The History of the Colony of New Sweden. *The Pennsylvania Magazine of History and Biography, 8*(2), 129–159. JSTOR.

Steinberg, J. (2013). *Bismarck: A Life*. Oxford University Press.

Stephan, R. (2019). Christina | queen of Sweden. In *Encyclopædia Britannica*. https://www.britannica.com/biography/Christina-queen-of-Sweden

Sturluson, S. (n.d.). *Heimskringla*. Wikisource. Retrieved December 23, 2022, from https://en.wikisource.org/wiki/Heimskringla/Saga_of_Sigurd_the_Crusader_and_His_Brothers_Eystein_and_Olaf

Tarling, N. (1966). *Southeast Asia, Past and Present*. F. W. Cheshire.

Taschner, J. C. (1968, January 21). *Nuclear Weapon Accident Near Thule Air Base, Greenland*. https://www.osti.gov/opennet/servlets/purl/1735362.pdf

Thomas, N. (2014). *Hitler's Blitzkrieg Enemies 1940: Denmark, Norway, Netherlands & Belgium*. Bloomsbury Publishing.

Þorgilsson, A. (2006). *Íslendingabok Kristni Saga - The Book of the Icelanders - The Story of the Conversion* (A. Faulkes & A. Finlay, Eds.; S. GRØNLIE, Trans.). Viking Society for Northern Research University College.

Trueman, C. N. (2015, March 25). *Gustavus Adolphus and Sweden*. History Learning Site. https://www.historylearningsite.co.uk/the-thirty-years-war/gustavus-adolphus-and-sweden/

United States Holocaust Memorial Museum. (2021a, July 7). *Raoul Wallenberg and the Rescue of Jews in Budapest*. Ushmm.org. https://encyclopedia.ushmm.org/content/en/article/raoul-wallenberg-and-the-rescue-of-jews-in-budapest

United States Holocaust Memorial Museum. (2021b, October 25). *Norway*. Ushmm.org; United States Holocaust Memorial Museum, Washington, DC. https://encyclopedia.ushmm.org/content/en/article/norway

Visit Ghana. (n.d.). *Visit Ghana - Christiansborg (Osu) Castle*. Visit Ghana. https://visitghana.com/attractions/christiansborg-osu-castle/

Walker, B. (2001, April 30). *Three cheers for Balkanization!* Www.enterstageright.com. http://www.enterstageright.com/archive/articles/0501balkanization.htm

Wangel, C.-A. (1982). *Sveriges militära beredskap 1939-1945*. Militärhistoriska Förlaget.

Waples, R. K., Hauptmann, A. L., Seiding, I., Jørsboe, E., Jørgensen, M. E., Grarup, N., Andersen, M. K., Larsen, C. V. L., Bjerregaard, P., Hellenthal, G., Hansen, T., Albrechtsen, A., & Moltke, I. (2021). The genetic history of Greenlandic-European contact.

Current Biology, *31*(10). https://doi.org/10.1016/j.cub.2021.02.041

Weber, C. (2019, January 31). *Hungarian & Finnish Evolved From This Common Language*. ThoughtCo. https://www.thoughtco.com/hungarian-and-finnish-1434479#:~:text=One%20of%20the%20most%20obvious

Wilson, W. A. (1976). *Open Indiana | Indiana University Press*. Open Indiana | Indiana University Press. https://publish.iupress.indiana.edu/read/folklore-and-nationalism-in-modern-finland/section/770d1e97-08c2-4878-8514-0dc4ed2f2b59

Zamoyski, A. (2009). *Poland: A History*. HarperCollins UK.

Zamoyski, A. (2012). *1812: Napoleon's Fatal March on Moscow*. HarperCollins UK.

Zamoyski, A. (2018). *Napoleon: A Life*. Basic Books.

FREE BONUS FROM HBA: EBOOK BUNDLE

Greetings!

First of all, thank you for reading our books. As fellow passionate readers of History and Mythology, we aim to create the very best books for our readers.

Now, we invite you to join our VIP list. As a welcome gift, we offer the History & Mythology Ebook Bundle below for free. Plus you can be the first to receive new books and exclusives! <u>Remember it's 100% free to join.</u>

Simply scan the QR code to join.

OTHER BOOKS BY HISTORY BROUGHT ALIVE

Available now in Ebook, Paperback, Hardcover, and Audiobook in all regions.

For Kids:

SCANDINAVIAN HISTORY

We sincerely hope you enjoyed our new book *"Scandinavian History"*. We would greatly appreciate your feedback with an honest review at the place of purchase.

First and foremost, we are always looking to grow and improve as a team. It is reassuring to hear what works, as well as receive constructive feedback on what should improve. Second, starting out as an unknown author is exceedingly difficult, and Amazon reviews go a long way toward making the journey out of anonymity possible. Please take a few minutes to write an honest review.

Best regards,
History Brought Alive
http://historybroughtalive.com/

www.ingramcontent.com/pod-product-compliance
Lightning Source LLC
Chambersburg PA
CBHW070553010526
44118CB00012B/1305